Have You Ever...
Bringing Literature to Life Through Creative Dramatics

Easy to use creative dramatics
lessons for well-known
stories and poems

By Lois Kipnis and Marilyn Gilbert

Alleyside Press

Published by Alleyside Press, an imprint of Highsmith Press
Highsmith Press
W5527 Highway 106
PO Box 800
Fort Atkinson, WI 53538-0800
1-800-558-2110

Copyright ©1994 by Lois Kipnis and Marilyn Gilbert

The purchase of this book entitles the individual librarian or teacher to reproduce copies for use in the library or classroom. The reproduction of any part for an entire school system or for commercial use is strictly prohibited. No form of this work may be reproduced or transmitted or recorded without written permission from the publisher.

"Mark's Fingers" and "Abigail's Fingers" (*Fingers Are Always Bringing Me News*, by Mary O'Neill. Doubleday, 1969) are reprinted by permission of International Creative Management, Inc. Copyright ©1969 by Mary O'Neill.
"The Snowman" (*Stories to Dramatize*, by Winifred Ward. New Orleans: Anchorage Press) is reprinted by permission of Anchorage Press.
"The Theft of Thor's Hammer" (*Norse Myths*, by Ingri and Edgar P. D'Aulaire. Doubleday)
Pierre copyright ©1962 by Maurice Sendak. All rights reserved. Used with permission.
Where the Wild Things Are copyright © 1963 by Maurice Sendak. All rights reserved. Used with permission.

Printed in the United States of America.

ISBN 0-913853-33-X

This book is dedicated to Dr. Hannah Masterson, who, through her gift of connecting artists and educators, and her belief in enriching the lives of children through the arts, made this book possible.

Our thanks also go to the many children whose enthusiastic participation has helped us shape our ideas; and to the administrators and teachers who provided support and encouragement to make our vision a reality.

Thanks also go to our families for their support and belief in our creative connection.

Contents

Preface 7

Introduction 9

How to Use Our **Have You Ever…** Lessons 12

How to Create Your Own **Have You Ever…** Lessons 14

Warm-ups 15

Have You Ever gotten something you wanted very badly, and found it was not what you wanted at all?
   Poem: "The Snow Man," Author Unknown 20

Have You Ever had to do something that was important but really boring... and you couldn't get out of doing it?
   "The Boy Who Cried Wolf," by Aesop 23

Have You Ever known someone who is always playing tricks, and to whom you'd love to teach a lesson?
   Anansi and the Moss-Covered Rock, an African folktale retold by Eric A. Kimmel 26

Have You Ever wondered how many different things you can do with your hands and fingers?
   Poems: "Abigail's Fingers," "Mark's Fingers," by Mary O'Neill 29

Have You Ever hoped so much for something and then been disappointed?
   Poem: "Casey at the Bat," by Ernest Lawrence Thayer 33

Have You Ever woken up on the wrong side of the bed, and no matter what you do, everything goes wrong?
   Where the Wild Things Are by Maurice Sendak 36

Have You Ever wanted or needed something badly but you were not able to convince anyone to give you what you wanted?
   "The Grasshopper and the Ant," by Aesop 39

Have You Ever been afraid to tell the truth because of the consequences?
   "The Emperor's New Clothes" 42

Have You Ever imagined what it would be like if your most valuable possession were missing?
   "The Theft of Thor's Hammer," in *Norse Myths* by the D'Aulaires 44

Have You Ever wondered about how you could resolve an argument without physical force?
   "The Sun and the Wind," by Aesop 46

Have You Ever been told to stop daydreaming?
    "The Peddler and His Caps" 49

Have You Ever wondered what it would be like if everything you touched turned to gold?
    "King Midas and the Golden Touch" 51

Have You Ever wondered what it would be like to be a bridge and be traveled over day after day?
    "The Three Billy Goats Gruff" 53

Have You Ever known someone who does not care about anyone else's feelings?
    Pierre by Maurice Sendak 54

Have You Ever imagined or wished you were strong enough to lift even the heaviest of boulders?
    "Hercules and the Twelve Labors" 56

Have You Ever been so lost in your dreams that you didn't pay any attention to what was going on?
    "The Milkmaid," by Aesop 57

Have You Ever with Nursery Rhymes
    "Humpty Dumpty," "Little Miss Muffet," "The Three Little Kittens," "Twinkle Twinkle Little Star," "Little Boy Blue," "Old King Cole," "Jack and Jill," "To Market, To Market" 59

Have You Ever wished that you could have all your wishes come true?
    "Aladdin" 65

Have You Ever been so curious that you'd risk anything to satisfy your curiosity?
    "Pandora's Box" 68

Have You Ever had a parent or teacher warn you not to do something, but you decided to do it anyway?
    "Daedalus and Icarus/Theseus and the Minotaur" 72

Have You Ever wondered what it would be like to have the stories and poems in the library come to life?
    Assorted stories and poems 76

Bibliography 77

Preface

Our book, *Have You Ever...*, is a guide designed to enable teachers to bring stories and poetry to life with their students through drama. Our introductory chapter will show you not only how to use the activities but how you can create your own *Have You Ever...* lessons using your favorite literature and poetry.

Note from Lois

For many years, I have been working as a drama consultant. I have conducted teacher training workshops and have worked with drama in the gifted classroom, heterogeneous classroom, and the special education classroom.

Wherever I have gone, I have met primary and elementary school teachers, librarians, and specialists who have expressed an interest in using drama with students, but who don't know how to begin, are afraid due to inexperience, or are in need of new material. I have suggested activities and have supplied bibliographies for these teachers, *but many were unable to take that initial step.* I realized that what teachers need is a step by step guide to show them how to do a complete drama activity from warm up to follow-up. I realized that a teacher needs a book that can be picked up and used immediately and successfully, with no background in drama. I tested the idea with Marilyn, and her students, for eight years. It proved to be successful, and therefore this book.

Note from Marilyn

Lois was a drama consultant in my school for eight years. Recently I began a program of schoolwide enrichment, K-6, including special education, and gifted and talented students. Confronted with the challenge of creating an appropriate enrichment curriculum, I turned to "Lois' Magic," Drama, with an extraordinarily positive reaction from classroom teachers.

I have also done extensive in-service training and have found that teachers of all kinds—Reading Teachers, Classroom Teachers, English as a Second Language Teachers, Library Media Specialists and others—are very interested in using drama as a tool in their classroom, but don't know how to begin. Whole language and cooperative learning approaches provide excellent opportunities for teachers to use drama in the classroom. *Have You Ever...* with its connection to fine children's literature, and its step by step approach, ensures that teachers can pick up our book and immediately begin involving their students in quality drama experiences. It is a practical guide, in which we have distilled theatre education theory into practice.

Our Note

In addition to the step by step, easy to follow format, what makes our book different is that it is not just a rehashing and modification of old theatre games, improvisations and story dramatizations. It is, instead, focused on stories and poems (some old, some new) with *original* approaches that have evolved based on the authors' experience and imagination.

- For the teacher who wants to use drama in the curriculum and classroom, but who has no background or experience in drama, we have developed a step by step format that is easy to understand and easy to use.
- For the *experienced* teacher and drama specialist, the material is new, exciting, and easily incorporated into your own style or method.

Each *Have You Ever....* lesson captures the basic concept of the story or poem, and relates it to the children's experience. Each *Have You Ever....* lesson has follow-up activities that relate to the curriculum.

The step by step approach guides you the teacher through each lesson, and provides follow-up activities and suggestions which then encourage your creativity to emerge.

Good luck, and have fun!

Introduction

Have you ever wanted to teach drama, but didn't know how to begin?
Have you ever wanted to take a story or poem and make it come alive?
Have you ever wanted a new and creative approach to your existing drama or language arts program?

Our book, *Have You Ever...*, will teach you how, and give you the confidence to try. The easy to follow, step by step lessons are the result of years of experimentation with drama in the elementary school classroom. We began many years ago with theatre games—and were thrilled along with the children at the excitement and creativity they engendered. We kept refining our approach, looking for ways to integrate this thrill and excitement into the "regular" curriculum. But we wanted more. We wanted drama to be a vehicle for teaching content areas, as well as an end in itself. We believe that the most meaningful kind of learning occurs through doing, and that drama is an excellent medium through which you can teach all kinds of subject matter, particularly language arts.

"Tell me, I will forget.
Show me, I might remember.
Involve me, I will understand."

Accordingly, we have developed a series of *Have You Ever...* creative dramatics lessons that can be infused into an existing language arts curriculum. Each lesson is based on a story or poem, and by using our dialogues, our voice will guide you through the lessons with suggestions for follow-up activities and room for your own creative ideas. The *Have You Ever...* question at the start of each lesson captures the attention of the children and focuses on a concept for discussion in a story or poem. It can be asked rhetorically, as a lead into the story or poem, or as a springboard for discussion before you begin the lesson. You can follow our step by step dialogues closely, or use them as a springboard for your own ideas.

Then on to the exercise itself. Drama excites children, and arouses their interest in literature. When children experience literature through drama in our *Have You Ever...* lessons they not only develop an understanding and appreciation for theme, character, plot and setting of the story they are involved with, they are motivated to read more. After doing the *Have You Ever...* lessons "Thor and His Hammer," and "Hercules and His Twelve Labors," a group of fourth graders eagerly went to the library to get collections of additional Norse and Greek myths. At the conclusion of the *Have You Ever...* fable lessons, third and fourth graders brought fable collections to school to read. After the "Anansi and the Moss-Covered Rock" story was dramatized, first graders excitedly went to the library for more "Anansi" folk tales.

By acting out our *Have You Ever...* lessons, dramatizing a story or a poem, children develop the ability to sequence events and to understand the structure of a story or the pattern of a poem. The children also develop the ability to think creatively, to become fluent and flexible thinkers. To use convincing and persuading, for example, activities that we introduce into many of our *Have You Ever...* lessons, the children learn to evaluate situations, express themselves clearly, communicate their ideas, think on their feet, problem solve, use language creatively and appropriately, increase vocabulary, and solve problems using new and different approaches. Clearly, these are the higher level thinking skills which we want all students to have the opportunity to develop.

Our lessons provide a safe environment not only for experimentation but for developing understanding of others. Through playing the roles of the characters in stories and poems, children gain insight into different kinds of people. Children can "try on" different personalities. They can slip into the skins of different people and learn empathy as they try to understand how they feel, or why they feel and behave in certain ways. Our lessons provide a safe environment for shy children to learn to be more assertive. In one class, a very shy boy, who took months to feel comfortable expressing himself in drama, volunteered to play the part of a "cool dude" in a story. Drama gave him a place to try on and test that character. We have seen other shy children shock their teachers with their vocal and verbal abilities in a drama situation—safely hidden behind "their character." We have seen a child who stutters portray the role of Zeus in "Pandora's Box" flawlessly and powerfully.

We have incorporated a great deal of pantomime into many of our *Have You Ever...* lessons. Pantomime contributes to children's ability to focus on sensory awareness and to note details. Their ability to do so enables them to make characters and situations come alive. The more familiar with pantomime children become, the more they focus on sensory awareness and details, skills important to the writing process, as well.

Our *Have You Ever...* lessons are geared to all children, from "regular," to special education, to gifted. In our extensive work with all these groups, drama has taught them how to focus on a task over time, has developed their feelings of achievement and pride in their accomplishments, and fostered their feeling of self-esteem and confidence. In addition, as the children work as a group to focus on the task of bringing literature alive, they learn how to interact with each other and work cooperatively to solve common problems. They learn to listen to each other and develop respect for each other's ideas. They laugh and enjoy together. Freed from the need to be right, the students feel safe and successful.

It was a challenge for us to designate grade level recommendations for our lessons. We have been as successful with "Humpty Dumpty," for example, on the sixth grade level, as in Kindergarten. We present the material so that there's room for it to be different each time according to the responses of each group. The experiences the children bring to it as they participate make it age appropriate. As the professional, you can be the judge. If a lesson seems appealing to you, at any grade level, and appropriate for your class, try it. Or, alter the vocabulary or approach to suit your grade level.

You may choose to do the *Have You Ever...* lessons in segments, or as a whole, depending on the time available and attention span of your students. Sometimes the children get so involved that the drama experience goes on for several periods for many days. The follow-ups provided can be done at a later time, or not at all, if you choose. You may even choose to use the follow-up activities at any time without the use of the *Have You Ever...* lessons.

To use *Have You Ever...* simply pick up the lesson and read it. Let your students "fill in the places" where there's room for them to act and be creative. Voilà. Creative dramatics from warm up games to follow-up activities. The best kind of learning is learning by doing—not only for the children, but for you as well.

We have provided a section on how to create your own *Have You Ever...* lessons. Our experience is that once teachers try our lessons, they want to create their own. We have also provided a bibliography for your future reference. Once you've tried *Have You Ever...* and have a feel for the structure and pace of a drama lesson, it will become exciting to consult other drama literature for more ideas. Having "done" drama, reading about it becomes really meaningful and exciting. You will note that we have a few lessons ("Thor," "Hercules," "Aladdin") that are not scripted "word for word." We merely guided you through the story with suggested activities and left you room to try adding your own "Have You Ever..." words.

A word about flops. They even occur on Broadway, in the glare of incredible publicity! If this kind of activity is very new to your students, and to you, have patience. No matter how many times we've tried our *Have You Ever...* lessons, sometimes we encounter a group with which a particular lesson just doesn't work. We believe that the most meaningful kind of learning, for you, as well as for your students, is through doing. Keep trying, the results will be worth it.

We hope that you and your classes will get as much enjoyment, excitement and imaginative fun as we have had from our *Have You Ever...* lessons.

How to Use Our *Have You Ever...* Lessons

You can use "Have You Ever..." lessons in many different ways. If you are comfortable using drama with students, you can plunge right in, and follow any one of the step by step lessons as they are written with your students. Or you can modify them to meet your needs.

If you prefer to acquaint your class with drama gradually before beginning with the lessons, we provide you with introductory, warm-up drama activities, appropriate for grades K-6.

Teachers tend to be concerned about discipline during drama. In reality, class control is relatively easy because working with drama is so motivating. The children are eager to cooperate, so maintaining discipline is actually very simple, especially if you establish and practice these three important guidelines with your class before you begin:

1. **Special space:** Explain to the students that many times all of them will be working at the same time, and will need a special space. This is a space where the child can stand and put arms out in front, in back and to the sides without touching anyone else.

    "It is as if there are invisible walls which let each of you work without seeing anyone else (although you really can!). It's your own special space to do your own creative thinking."

    Practice finding a special space quickly and quietly.

2. **Freeze and focus:** It is really important to be able to get the children's attention immediately during a drama activity without a lot of fuss. We use a drumbeat, but you can use whatever signal you like. A bell, a pot lid and stick, etc. all work as long as they are used consistently. When the class hears your drumbeat (or your selected signal) they must *instantly* freeze and focus. Explain that "freeze" means to make no movement (like a statue) and no sound. "Focus" means that the children should focus their eyes on you, as they freeze, for further directions.

    It is best to practice using the signal several times during the first drama session to firmly establish how it works. To do so, have the children stand in a big circle, or near their desks, or in their special space. "Let's all stand in a big circle. Let's shake loose our hands, add in the elbows, shoulders, head, neck, knees, feet, etc. When I beat the drum, I want everyone to freeze and focus."

    "Good. Now, let's try it again. This time, let's be wicked witches. Let's see you show how witch-like you can be with your body. Let's start with your wrists, hands, elbows, shoulders, neck, face, etc. When I beat the drum, freeze into the ugliest witches you can, and focus on me." Beat the drum.

    Repeat as needed having the children be rubber people, aliens, etc.

3. **Actor/audience rule:** Explain to the class that there is a rule in drama called the "actor/audience rule." It means that when an actor or group of actors is performing, the children who are the audience have the responsibility to sit quietly and focus on them. If they hear you say "audience rule" while someone is acting, it is a reminder that someone has forgotten to focus on the actor. (Saying "audience rule" is more positive and successful than having to say "be quiet," etc.)

Your role as the teacher using warm-ups and lessons

Your role throughout the "Have You Ever..." warm up and lesson is to guide the activity; to help focus it. Everything you need to say is scripted right in, but do not be afraid to depart from the format (especially as you gain confidence). For example, you can step in as a character, or as an interviewer who asks a question, to help give a scene a focus. This role will become easier as you do it.

As the students are acting, many times all you will need to do is to coach from the sidelines as a means of reinforcing concentration and offering help. Some useful words or phrases are: "Focus," "Concentrate," "Keep it real," "We want to believe the character/feeling," "What else could you do?" "Use your face and body to show us how you feel."

Suggestions

When: You can do a lesson

- when you are reading a particular fable or story.
- when you are focusing on a certain kind of literature (fables, myths, etc.).
- once a week, at a time set aside for "Have You Ever..." activities.
- daily, for 10 or 15 minutes, working on one section at a time, so that by the end of a week an activity is completed.

Who: We found it difficult to suggest ages/grade levels for each "Have You Ever..." You, the teacher, are the best judge of appropriateness for your class. Sometimes simplifying a direction or changing the vocabulary opens activities to your students. We have had no problem using "younger" literature with the older students—the activities become more sophisticated by virtue of what the students bring to them.

How to Create Your Own *Have You Ever...* Scripted Lessons

After you have used our lessons, you can create your own "Have You Ever..." lessons to fit your curricular needs. Follow the format we have used.

Decide on a poem or story. Determine how to relate the theme to the students' experiences: "Have you ever…"

Use the theme as the basis for determining everyday or fantasy situations relating to it for the students to role play as warm ups. If you wanted to use "The Emperor's New Clothes," for example, one of the themes is the avoidance of truth in order to save face. For this story, the "Have You Ever..." might be: "Have you ever been afraid to admit the truth because of the consequences?" Brainstorm for contemporary situations the students could create to dramatize.

Characters—determine who else might be in the story. How could you change the story to add different characters? (What would the Emperor's mother say about her son and this situation?)

Point of View—through whose eyes other than the main character could you see this story—what new twist or focus could you give to it? (What made the tailors think they could get away with the hoax? If we could interview them, what might you ask; what might they say? Why did the child tell the truth? Why didn't the other townspeople? The members of the court?)

Conflict—what is it, and how could it be made to relate to the students' lives? (If the boy in the story tells his friends that he will tell the truth the next day will his friends try to talk him out of it? What are some situations where a person could be talked out of telling the truth?)

Improvisation—find one or two sentences to focus on in the story or poem that will spark improvisational scenes. (The Emperor loved clothes, and people came from all over to sell clothing to him. Different kinds of merchants/tailors, maybe from other countries, come to court to try to sell him various items.)

Pantomime—determine how pantomime can be used to set the scene for the story. (How do the townspeople react to the Emperor's new outfit on the day of the parade? How can we make believe we are sewing, cutting, and designing clothing using imaginary cloth?)

Unanswered questions—if you could, what would you like to know that was not included in the story?

Follow-up activities—using our ideas as guides, create writing, art, music, etc. experiences for your students.

Student creators—share the "Have You Ever..." formula with your students, and have the whole class or the more adept students create their own lessons.

Warm-ups

Here are some easy warm-ups you can use either as self-contained activities or as introductory activities for the longer "Have You Ever..." lessons. We have integrated "side coaching," or cues to the students, into the warm-ups.

Non-verbal warm-ups

Sometimes a Kindergarten or first grade class (or the teacher) needs a simpler, more concrete introduction to pantomime before trying the activities described below. If so, you may wish to try the "Beach Ball Introduction."

Start with the children in a circle and a real beach ball. Pass the ball around the circle. Tell the children that even after the ball has gone to the next student, they should pretend that they are still holding the ball.

"Show with your hands and bodies that you are still holding the ball. Show how you would bounce that ball. Focus on the imaginary ball, and make it seem real."

"Now pretend that the ball is shrinking, and show with your hands and bodies that it's becoming a tiny, hard bouncing ball. Now it's growing into a soccer ball—show how you use it. Now it's a small but very heavy ball, that is not such a good bouncer. Now it's baseball sized, and extremely sticky. Show what happens when you try to throw it," etc.

Pantomime #1

"Have you ever wondered how you could enter some exciting contests and win trophies without ever leaving this room? Well, you can. With your imagination and through pantomime (the art of acting with no words, no sounds, no objects or props) you can be anywhere and do anything."

"Everyone, find a special space. Ready? The first contest we're going to enter is The Annual Bubble Gum Bubble Blowing Contest. There's a trophy for the one who can blow the biggest bubble. The judges are not ready yet. While they're getting ready, take an imaginary piece of gum out of your pocket. Think of where your pocket is. Think of how you will unwrap the gum. What will you do with the wrapper? Put the gum into your mouth and chew it. Hmm, maybe you need a second piece. Take it out of your pocket, unwrap it, put it in your mouth. Now chew it, and get it good and soft and ready for a good bubble."

"The judges are ready now, and I am going to be one of them."

"Get on your mark, get set, go. Blow that bubble. Focus on the bubble. See it getting bigger, and bigger, and bigger, and bigger, and bigger until...oh no, it popped! It's all over your face! Let me really believe you're taking the gum off your face. As you are doing it, show me how you feel because you lost the contest."

"Freeze."

"Well, you didn't win that contest, but you're not the kind of person to give up, so you decide to enter the next contest, The Worldwide Weight Lifting Contest. You will be judged on three things:

> One, how slowly and gracefully you lift the weights from the ground to over your head.
> Two, how long you can hold the weights over your head.
> Three, how gracefully and slowly you can bring the weights back down to the floor."

"The judges aren't quite ready. While they're getting ready, stretch those bodies—get your bodies warmed up for a good weight lifting session. Flex your arms, your hands, move your backs, do some deep knee bends. What else can you think of to do to get ready? You'd really love to get that trophy to show off to all of your friends."

"OK, the judges are ready. I will be one of them. On your mark, get set (remember, this is pantomime, so *no sounds!*), go! Slowly, carefully, lift those weights up. Now let's see how long you can hold the weights over your head. It's getting heavier and heavier, but don't give up. *(Have the students try to hold the positions for a few seconds, and add the following)*:

Oh, no! You just got an itch on your stomach. What an awful time to get an itch. What will you do? Ah! The itch has gone. Now, slowly, gently, bring the weights down.

Stand up, loosen up your body as you wait for the announcement of the winner. Show me in pantomime how you feel when you find out that you just won the Worldwide Weight Lifting Contest.

Well, you've won one trophy. You've decided to enter one last contest before you go home. This contest is The International Balancing the Book On Your Head Contest. The judges are ready.

Carefully place a book (imaginary) on your head. Let me see by the way you use your hands how thick it is, and how big or small, light or heavy. The judges now say "Go." Really feel that book on your head as you walk around your special space. You're not allowed to touch it, even if it starts to slip and fall. Careful! (Let them walk a bit, and then add): Oh, no! You have an urge to sneeze. Try to control that urge, or you may lose that book on your head. Ah, the urge to sneeze has passed. What other obstacles to success might you have? (i.e. gum stuck on your shoe, etc.)

Now the judges want to see you walk back to your seat and actually sit down with that book balanced on your head. Careful, careful. (When they have done this): Good, now they have announced that you have all won a trophy for outstanding performance in The International Balancing the Book on Your Head Contest. Congratulations, you have two trophies to take home today."

Students may have other ideas for contests to pantomime. *(For example, a pie eating contest, a juggling contest, etc.)*

Pantomime #2

"Have you ever looked forward to a special treat? Well, today's the day! Your friend's grandfather has been the head of costumes for all the top New York plays and big movies, and he's invited you to spend a day with him at the costume warehouse where he works. There are all kinds of costumes, hats, jewelry, props, masks, etc., and he's given you permission to try things on and pretend to be different characters."

"Let's all go to our special spaces. Imagine you all have a mirror in front of you so you can try to look at yourself in each costume you try on. Really focus on your image in the mirror. See if you can really become the character the costume suggests."

"Some costumes are in boxes, some in old dusty trunks, some hanging on racks. You decide the details, but really let us see how you get the costume out, and how you put it on. Think of the way you'd put it on if you zip it, if you button it. Feel the fabric it's made of. Is it a red velvet king's robe? Is the hat very large, with a big feather on it? Every possible costume is there, from witches clothes, to princess dresses, to pirate hats *(you supply further descriptive details, as desired)*."

"Really concentrate on your own outfit, and your image in the mirror. Don't look at anyone else. This is your special time to really see and believe in what you're doing. Keep on trying different things. As I walk around, your pantomime should help me really see what you're wearing."

"OK, Go!"

(As you walk around, side-coaching comments such as "Focus" and "Really see what you're putting on," "Don't forget from where you're taking the costume," etc., will be helpful to the students.)

(You may wish to end with:) "Now, let's try the mask box. These masks were made by a world-famous mask-maker. Let's find a happy-face mask. Think of how it will go on—does it tie? Does it have elastic? Put it on. Look at yourself in the mirror. Now take it off. Try on different masks (angry, sad, etc.)."

"Now you try on the scariest mask of all. Oh, no! It gets stuck on your face and...."

Pantomime #3

"This time you will try some pantomimes using your five senses. Let's have four or five of you in the chairs in front of the room. Each of you will do three different pantomimes for each of our five senses." *(Use volunteers.)*

"OK, let's start with the sense of seeing. Let's imagine you're in a movie theatre and you are watching a very scary movie. Really concentrate and see it on the screen. Think of how you would act. Do you have popcorn? Anything else? Remember, it's pantomime, so no sounds. Let us see you watching that movie." *(Give the children time to act.)*

"Here it is, the scariest scene you've ever seen—it's the scene the whole school is talking about."

"Now, instead of the scariest movie, you're watching the funniest movie you've ever seen."

"Now, you're watching a live baseball game. The score is 0–0. It's the bottom of the 9th inning. Your team is up at bat. If your team scores a run, not only do you win the game, but you are the champions! Show us in pantomime how tense you are—focus on the batter."

"OK, the pitcher is throwing the ball." *(Call out the play by play and the students respond in pantomime. Maybe the player gets to second base, and another player is up, etc.)*

"Finally as the player gets to home base, show in pantomime whether your team won or not."

(These students go back to the audience. Four or five new students come up. Use the same format for each sense. Here are some suggestions, or you can use the students' ideas.)

Taste:
Sour lemon—focus on details, pits, size of the lemon, if some gets in the student's eye, etc.
Pizza—it's hot, there may be too much cheese or hot pepper, etc.
Caramel candy—it gets stuck in your tooth, and you're in the library, and not supposed to be eating.

Touch:
A splinter— being removed from your finger by an imaginary person. Be sure to include the details of the splinter being removed, even after it's out.
A large, beautiful feather—show how big and soft it is, and all of the things you can do with it.
Sand—build a sand castle. You may want to use the dribble method or the pack in the sand method. Imagine a Martian is watching you. Show how it is done step by step. Focus on the details of the castle, the feel of the sand, of too much mud on your hands, etc.

Smell:
Campfire—roasting marshmallows over a fire, suddenly a skunk comes along.

Baking—you have just come home from school and someone has made your favorite chocolate chip cookies. You sneak a cookie from the plate. Really smell it.

Flowers—you are in a flower garden, picking a lovely bouquet of flowers to surprise someone. Focus on from where you get the flowers —a tree, a bush, the ground. What are you putting the flowers in—a basket, a vase, your other hand, etc. Let us see you sniffing the flowers as you pick them. Some of them smell great, some don't.

Hearing:

A bee—buzzing around you, a mosquito, a fly.

Calls—different people on the phone—a boring older relative, a good, juicy gossipy story, etc.

Music—you are wearing headphones, and you hear different kinds of music —rap, rock, classical, etc.

Verbal Warm-ups

Verbal Warm-up #1—Persuasion

Have the students seated on the floor or in chairs in a circle.

"Have you ever wanted something so badly that you *never* give up the idea of getting it? Well, let's try to imagine that your best friend's dog just had puppies, and your friend wants to give you one—*free*! You've just come and asked me, your parent, if you can have the dog. I've said 'No.'"

"Now, one at a time, I want each one of you to say something that will convince me to let you have the puppy. The challenge is, that once a person has said something or tried a certain approach, it cannot be repeated. Remember what persuade means." *(Have the students define it.)* "Try as many different things you can to persuade me, to convince me that you should have that puppy. Give reasons, work out solutions. Who would like to start?"

Verbal Warm-up #2—Conflict Improvisations

"Get a partner, and sit with that partner so that both of you have a special space."

"Decide on a situation where each of you wants something else. *(Friends with different ideas of how to spend the day. A student who wants to convince a teacher of something the teacher doesn't want to do, etc. Additional ideas below.)*

"Do not act out the situation. Just decide who you are, and what the conflict will be." *(Teacher goes around to groups to check ideas, helping where necessary.)*

"Now, let's take turns acting out each scene. As you are working out the conflict, really try to persuade the other person to see the situation your way. Do not give in right away, so that each person has to keep trying to convince the other." *(Teacher can call "Freeze" to stop the action at any point.)*

Possible situations:

Brothers or sisters who want to watch different TV shows.

Teenager wants to go out, parent says "No," s/he has to baby-sit for a younger brother or sister.

One child has a toy or game and is unwilling to share with the other.

Baby-sitter wants a child to go to sleep, but the child wants to stay up.

Child wants outrageous hairdo or new outrageous fashion item or style, parent says "No."

Two siblings, one of whom wants to go on a scary amusement park ride, and the other is afraid and wants to go on the merry go round. A parent has said that you both *must* go on the ride together.

Child wants to go somewhere with friends. Parent insists his/her room must be cleaned first. The room is a disaster and will take forever.

Two friends, students or siblings both want the same chair for story time, or the same seat at the dinner table.

Parent wants the child to go to visit an elderly relative for the afternoon. The child does not want to go. S/he had made other, more interesting plans.

You have four more boxes of Girl Scout Cookies to sell to win the new bicycle. The only one who is home is the older brother or sister who is not interested. Convince him or her!

Note: *After you have done a few of these conflict situations, define for the students the terms Improvisation and Role Playing.*

"What you have done is called improvisation. You did not plan what you were going to say. You found out who you were supposed to be, where you were, and what you wanted; but, you created the dialogue and improvised as you went along. You also just did what is called "Role Play." That is, you played (or acted), a particular role—parent, child, friend, teacher, etc. When you do that you have to think, act and feel as the person would in the role you're playing."

Follow-up activity

Children can brainstorm characters and situations, and create their own "Conflict Drama Kit" by writing them on cards for their classmates to use for improvisations at other times. Two students volunteer to act, pick a card, and improvise. The bibliography includes several resources for additional ideas for improvisations using conflict and persuasion.

The Snowman

HAVE YOU EVER gotten something you wanted very badly, and found it was not what you wanted at all?

"I have a poem to share with you about a snowman who wants to go into a house."

(Read "Snowman," author unknown, which appears at the end of this lesson.)

"Now, before we can act out the poem, let's build a snowman in pantomime. What do we need in order to build a snowman?"

"Let's be different kinds of snow. First show me what it would be like if you were slow, softly falling flakes, gently melting as you touch the ground. How about blizzard snow? Etc. How can we work together to create the storm?"

"Now, let's pretend we are walking through different kinds of snow: heavy, deep snow; light snow, that's just beginning to stick; a blizzard; hail; on ice." *(To avoid an immediate slip and fall for walking on ice, suggest that the child is holding a favorite toy in his or her hand.)*

"Now, we've got a good snowfall. You'd like to go outside to play, but your mother or father says 'No.' What possible reasons could they have? Try to convince your parent to let you go out." *(Challenge the students to come up with as many different reasons as possible.)* "What finally convinces your parent?"

"You've succeeded, so now we need to get dressed to go outside. What do we need? Working in your special space, let's pantomime putting on all the clothing you'll need to go outside (boots, etc.)."

"OK, let's go outside. Uh-oh, the door is hard to open, it's blowing so hard outside."

"Now, let's build the snowman."

"Let's build the body. Add the finishing touches. What do we need? (Hat, eyes, broom, scarf, etc.) Let's look at our snowman. Let's take a picture of him."

"Now, let's become the snowman. What shape are you? Show me with your body how you have become the snowman. Let's see how a happy snowman would look. A sad snowman. A lonely snowman because no other snow person is on the block. What other kinds of snow people could we be?" *(Have children brainstorm for other kinds of snowpeople, and show how each would look.)*

"Hello, I'm a reporter for the *Frosty Time News*. I'm here to ask each of you what it's like standing here day after day." *(Interview each one—or several, depending on the size of the class.)*

"What have you always wanted to ask a snowperson about his or her life?" Children can brainstorm for questions to ask. Questions may include: "What are your favorite decorations? When did you first notice the things around you, and realize what you were? What is your favorite weather? Why? How do you feel at night? Do you have a family? How do you stay in touch? How long do you expect to live? What happens to you in the spring? Where do you go in the summer? What do you think will happen to you next year? What have you been in your other lives? Where would you like to live best of all? Where would you like to go on vacation? What do the words 'safe and warm' mean to you?"

After the interviews are concluded:

"Suddenly we hear on the air, 'We interrupt this interview to bring you a special weather bulletin. A North Wind is heading this way. Take any precautions necessary.'"

"Snowman, maybe we could ask the North Wind to blow you inside the house!"

"Now half of us will be the North Wind, and half will be the snowmen. Snowmen, I want you, one at a time, to try to convince the North Wind to blow you inside. North Wind, you're not so sure you want to waste your breath on the snowmen, so really make them work hard convincing you."

(At some point, finally have the North Wind agree to blow the snowmen inside. Act it out. How would the snowmen react? What would they do? Build the scene to the climax where the snowmen finally melt into a puddle on the floor.)

"How would the wind react to all of this? The bed? Furniture?"

"What if the wind won't blow the snowman in—how else could he get inside?"

"What other wishes might the snowman have had other than wanting to go inside?" *(Act out.)*

"Do you think the snowman is sorry for his wish to go inside? Will he wish differently next time? Write a new poem with his new wish."

Follow this with some improvisations:

1. Your mother comes home, finds a puddle on the floor. Try to convince her that it was the snowman.
2. You're doing your homework and your mother went to the store and told you not to let anyone into the house. Suddenly a snowman arrives in your room.
3. You're the manager at Toys R Us. A snowman has just come through the door. What do you do? How would the dolls react? How would a little child in the store react. Suppose the parent s/he's with doesn't believe him or her. How would a grouchy shopper react? What else could happen?
4. You are a reporter on the spot. Interview people in the store, etc.

Follow-up activities

1. Act out a situation where you wished for something and it didn't meet your expectations.
2. Produce a Snowman Newspaper with news, advertisements, comics, etc. appropriate for snowmen.
3. Write a poem about wind, snow, winter.
4. Individually or in groups students create a snowman mail order catalogue, complete with illustrations. What items would you include? What prices would you charge? What would the name of your company be?
5. Create a snowman family photo album, complete with captions for the pictures. Consider colors, media that would convey/reflect a snowperson's taste.
6. Create a snowman's diary, describing life day by day from creation to melting.
7. Work on choral speaking with "The Snow Man."
8. Read and dramatize some additional poetry about snow and snowmen
   such as those from *It's Snowing, It's Snowing,* by Jack Prelutsky
9. Let's think of all the different activities we associate with winter. The children pantomime them singly or in groups. i.e., drinking hot cocoa, making a fire in the fireplace, shovelling snow, getting in and out of snow clothes—boots are a little too small, the zipper on your jacket gets stuck.

The Snow Man

(Author Unknown)

Once there was a Snow Man
Stood outside the door.
Thought he'd like to come inside
And run around the floor;
Thought he'd like to warm himself
By the firelight red,
Thought he'd like to climb
Upon the big white bed;
So he called the North Wind,
"Help me now I pray,
I'm completely frozen
Standing here all day."
So the North Wind came along
And blew him in the door—
Now there's nothing left of him
But a puddle on the floor.

The Boy Who Cried Wolf

(by Aesop)

HAVE YOU EVER
had to do something that was important but really boring... and you couldn't get out of doing it? How did you feel? How did you try to solve your problem?

"Let me share with you a story about a shepherd. This story is a fable. A fable is a short story that usually uses animals as the main characters and it teaches a lesson. In this story, the shepherd has an important job, but s/he finds it very boring."

"What is a shepherd boy or girl?"

(Tell or read the story.)

"Now, we're going to create a whole town of people, and each time the child cries 'wolf' three or four different characters will go to the top of the hill to see what's happening."

"First, though, before you become the townspeople, let's think about how different people act. Different people speak or walk or talk differently depending on who they are. For example, a shy person enters a room and says hello very differently than a proud king or queen. A very neat person eats potato chips differently than a sloppy person."

(Teacher elicits further examples and has students demonstrate.)

"How would you walk up the hill if you were very scared? or very daring? Let's try a few characters as examples." *(Can be done individually or in groups.)*

"We will have the shepherd boy or girl cry 'wolf' four or five times before the real wolf comes. Each time a different person will be the shepherd person."

"Let's start to set up the scene. Now for some townspeople. *(Here are some suggestions. You can elicit other ideas from the children.)*

Some suggestions for characters:

  a calm, kind, responsible adult
  a curious child, lover of nature, inquisitive
  a neat, squeamish, fussy lady or man
  a grouchy, irritable pizza maker
  a bored teen
  a daring, adventurous child
  a tough, take-charge sheriff, who believes in law and order
  the wealthiest, snobbiest man or woman in town
  a proud, older, retired shepherd
  an unhappy, sad, shy child
  a bossy teenager who always thinks s/he is right
  a careful, cautious professional spy
  a grouchy, old complaining person
  a mischievous six year old, a troublemaker
  a gossipy chatterbox
  a hermit who doesn't like people
  an impatient, rude person
  an efficient business person
  an overly protective worried parent
  a show-off, braggart

"Who would like to be the shepherd? A shy, nervous, scared, unadventurous 8 year old? A cool, tough bully? A happy, friendly child who loves to play, have fun, share and tell stories?"

"The townspeople wait till it's time for them to begin their parts."

"Now we'll start with the shepherd. Think about how you feel. Let's see you feed the sheep. Be sure to show us with details, in pantomime, from where you get the food."

"Talk to the sheep. Let them know how bored and lonely you feel. Speak your thoughts out loud."

"Let's see you try to think of different ideas of things you could do to add excitement to your life."

"Finally, let's hear you get the idea to pretend that there's a wolf attacking your sheep." *(Shepherd acts this out.)*

"Now, those of you who are the townspeople, after the shepherd calls wolf, you'll go to the top of the hill, one at a time. Each of you will come from a different part of the room."

"Think about your character. Think about how you'll go up the hill, one at a time. Think about how you would react to the shepherd. What would you say? Think of at least two questions your kind of character would ask the shepherd."

"Shepherd, when you're ready, cry 'wolf.'"

"People, do your part. React to the shepherd, ask questions."

"Shepherd, try to convince them that you really did see a wolf."

(Run the scene.)

(Before you tell the children to re-run the scene, as each group of three comes down from the hill, interview each one about what they saw and what they think about the situation. Could they suggest a solution to the problem?)

"What happened up there?"

"Do you think s/he's telling the truth?"

"Was there really a wolf?"

"Are you going to go back up there if he calls wolf again?" etc.

(Focus the children on how the character they are playing would respond.)

(Then, before you replay the scene, have the shepherd seriously consider whether or not to play the trick again. Have a good and bad conscience talking to him about whether or not to play the trick again.)

"Now, let's have the shepherd think about whether or not to play the trick again. Would someone be the shepherd's bad conscience talking to him/her? The good conscience?"

(Then reset the scene four or five times and run it each time with a different shepherd and different characters. Repeat interviews and consciences. Challenge each shepherd person to be different than the one before; to think of a different way to express boredom and loneliness. After everyone has had a chance to be a different character or shepherd, go around town to interview all or some of the characters the children played.)

"I want to see if your character feels the truth is being told."

"How can you tell if the shepherd is telling the truth?"

"Are you going back up there if he calls wolf again?"

(Focus the children on how the character they are playing would respond.)

"Before the real wolf comes, let's shift the scene to see what the sheep think about all this."

"Who would like to be a baby sheep?"

"Little baby sheep, how do you feel about what the shepherd is doing?"

"Who would like to be a Grampa or Grandma sheep?," etc.

(Same or additional questions as children decide.)

"What other kinds of sheep should we have?"

"Now this time, the real wolf is going to come. Who would like to be the wolf?"

"Let's think of how a wolf would walk and act. Remember, the wolf isn't interested in the shepherd boy. S/he just wants to fill his or her belly with sheep."

(Run the scene with the townspeople. This time, they are not responding to the cries of the shepherd.)
(The wolf leaves.)

"OK, shepherd, come down to town and tell the truth—describe what really happened on the hillside."

(Either end the story in the traditional manner or have the class decide on different ways the story could have ended, act out the suggestions. You may wish to spend some time discussing the moral of the story.)

Follow-up activities

1. Create a town newspaper. Have the articles focus on the incident. They can be straight news reports, interviews, etc. What would the name of the town be? The paper? What kinds of shops would there be that would place ads in the paper? What other kinds of local news would there be? What kinds of letters would there be to the advice columnist?

2. Do a news broadcast from the local TV or radio station, complete with interviews.

3. Tell the story from the wolf's point of view. What was he really doing on the mountain? Why did he attack the sheep?

4. The shepherd in the story lost his or her job after the incident. Conduct interviews for the replacement. What questions would you ask the candidates for the job? Run the interviews.

5. In small groups, come up with other solutions the shepherd could have used to relieve boredom. (i.e. sheep games, video games, etc.)

6. Create the scene at the Sheriff's office when the citizens are demanding that something be done about the shepherd; that the wolf be caught.

Anansi and the Moss-Covered Rock

(Our favorite version is the one retold by Eric A. Kimmel)

HAVE YOU EVER known someone who is always playing tricks and to whom you'd love to teach a lesson? Here is a story about a tricky spider who learns his lesson well.

"Every country has its favorite stories to tell, and in Africa, some of the favorite stories are about Anansi the Spider."

"Now, let me tell you a little about Anansi. He is like a very mischievous little boy who always likes to play tricks, and always ends up getting into trouble for his tricks. Anansi also loves to eat, but because he's so lazy, he is always playing tricks in order to get food."

"One of my favorite stories about Anansi is 'Anansi and the Moss-Covered Rock.'"

"Now, we're going to do two things. First, I'll read the story to you, and then we'll act out the story."

"I'll need your help as I'm reading the story. In our story there is a sentence that keeps being repeated: 'they went Walking—walking—walking.' Let's make it sound like a *slow* long walk through the hot forest. Let's try it together. Let's also try it to sound like a big elephant's steps: WALKING—WALKING—WALKING. Or, very fast like a spider. How many different ways can we make it sound?"

"There is another thing I need your help with. When the animals say 'Isn't this a strange moss-covered rock,' something happens. They fall down, and the sound is 'KPOM.' Let's try to say KPOM as if you fell down, hit your head, and are dizzy. How many different ways can we say it?"

"O. K. Now we're ready for the story."

(Teacher, read the story only up to the part where he plays the trick on all the animals. Do not read the ending yet.)

Scene One

"Now let's act out the story. Let's start with Anansi. Why do you think he's going for a walk in the forest? Is it to cool off? To meet a friend? To get food? To finish a web? Etc. Where are you before you go for a walk? *(Elicit responses.)* Show us where you are going and what you'll do when you get there."

"Let's have another spider friend. What would two spiders talk about? Let's hear the conversation. Finally, Anansi, you leave the house and go to the forest, and let's act out the scene between Anansi and the rock." [**Note:** A big cheerleader's pom pom, turned upside down, makes a great moss covered rock.]

"Anansi, when you reach the rock, let's hear your thoughts. Examine it."

"An hour passes. Anansi regains consciousness. Anansi, let's see you get up as if you're dizzy and can't figure out what happened to you. When you do realize what happened, let's hear your idea for your trick. Tell us your idea. Who would like to be Anansi's conscience, and try to talk him out of it?"

Scene Two

"Who would like to be Anansi? The lion? The lion's friend? What do you think two lions would be talking about? How do lions move? What are they eating? Maybe the lions have just heard that a lion tamer has come to look for lions, capture them, and tame them for a circus. How would the two lions be discussing it?"

(Play the scene.) "Perhaps Anansi is peeking over the fence, watching them, listening to them, salivating over the yams piled up high."

"Anansi now knocks at the door, visits them, and tries to convince them to go for a walk."

"As they take their walk, what are they thinking about? What do you think they are discussing? What kind of voices do they have."

"When you arrive at the rock, lion, really examine it *curiously*." *(Act out the KPOM scene.)*

"While lion is unconscious, spider runs to the lion's house and mimes getting the food. What do you put it in?" *(Each time have it differ: a barrel, a sack, a box, a wagon. Focus on detailed pantomime.)*

(End the scene with the lion regaining consciousness, getting home, and discovering his food is gone.) "Show us how he feels." *(Teacher, or student, you can interview him for the "Jungle News," about what happened.)*

(Repeat each scene using the same format:)

1. Two animals eating, talking, doing something.

2. Anansi convincing one to go with him for a walk.

3. The animal and Anansi walking, talking, etc.

4. The KPOM sequence and Anansi taking the food.

5. The ending—back home and interviewing.

Some suggestions:

The elephant could be bossy, ordering around a little mouse.
The giraffe could be snobbish.
The zebra could be an old grandpa or grandma zebra telling a baby zebra about all his/her adventures in the forest.
Consider adding any of the animals of an African jungle or forest.
You may want to use Orff instruments to accompany each animal's walk.

Scene Three

"Now, let's have a meeting of all the animals." *(Every one is in special space.)*

"Animals, what shall we do to solve this problem of our disappearing food? Each one raise your hand, and offer a suggestion." *(Elicit responses from the children: how do you think the story will end?)*

"O.K. Let's now see how the story ends." *(Read the story and then act out the ending. End it with a parade, instruments, etc., of all the animals miming carrying their food home.)*

"We've finished the story, but I have a question. Why is the rock magic? *Why* does it do what it does? *How* does it do it? Everyone go to your special spaces. Pretend you are the moss covered rock. Each one of you will share your secret with us." *(Some ideas children have had: I'm a magician disguised as a rock. I don't like to be insulted. It hurts my feelings when someone makes fun of me. I'm a bully underneath. A fairy put a spell on me, etc.)*

Follow-up activities

1. Write a story about Anansi's next trick.

2. When each animal is unconscious, what does s/he dream of? Write the story of his or her dream. Illustrate it.

3. Interview Anansi's family. What was he like as a child? How did he get to be the way he is now?

4. Interview Anansi's teachers and friends. What was he like as a youngster?

5. Write a radio or TV program about the "unsolved mystery" of the moss-covered rock. Act it out.

6. Read more Anansi stories and act them out.

7. Have Anansi write a letter of apology to each animal.

8. Have a testimonial dinner for bush deer. What would each animal bring bush deer for a present? Have each animal give a short testimonial speech.

Fingertalk

HAVE YOU EVER
wondered how many different things you can do with your hands and fingers? *(Elicit responses.)*

"Let's use our hands (and bodies) to do some pantomime today."

"Pantomime means acting without words, sounds, or real objects. We communicate with our faces and bodies."

Pantomime warm-ups:

Candy box mimes

"You have a box in front of you filled with all sorts of goodies. Think about the size of the box, and how it opens. I will know by how you use your hands how big it is, and how it opens. First reach in and take out a bag of potato chips. Think about how you will pick it up. Think about how you will open the bag. Take out a chip and eat it. Eat like a fussy person, like a teenager in a hurry, like a spoiled child."

"Now, reach in and take out a lollipop. Think about how it will be different than when you took out the potato chips. Think about how it's wrapped. Unwrap it, and eat it."

"Now take out your favorite candy bar. Think about how that will be different than it was before. Smell it. Think about how it's wrapped, and unwrap it. Eat it. It suddenly becomes very sticky. Then very hard. Then very crunchy."

"Reach in and take out some other 'goodies' of your own choice."

"Now the box disappears."

Action mimes

(Before the lesson, the teacher creates a set of cards with a different action written on each. One at a time, a student selects a card and pantomimes the action. When s/he has finished, the class guesses what the action is. If it's not clear to the class, challenge the actor to add more details to make it clear as to what s/he intended.)

Some suggestions for actions:

    blow up a balloon
    blow bubbles with a wand and soap solution from a jar
    shovel snow
    get a can of soda from a vending machine
    fly a kite
    play with a gerbil or hamster
    flip pancakes
    paint a picture
    eat very hot soup
    sweep the floor
    march in a parade

Passing the object

"Let's introduce some real objects." *(Pass around a simple object such as a cane, or a piece of fabric, etc. Each child must pantomime an action using the prop. In the case of the cane, children can use it for things such as a bat, a tennis racket, a toothbrush, etc. The fabric could be a shawl, a handkerchief, a dust cloth, etc. Both can be used together—the cane and fabric could be a flag, an umbrella, etc. When the child comes to a stop, the rest of the children may raise hands and guess what s/he was doing.)*

"Now let's read 'Abigail's Hands' and 'Mark's Fingers.' *(These poems appear at the end of the lesson.)* Let's make believe that we are Abigail's or Mark's fingers and hands. Their hands tell them what's hot and cold. Let's pretend to hold a cold ice cube in our hands. Now let's pretend to hold a hot piece of toast in our hands. What other things can we hold in our hands? What cold things? Sticky? Light? Heavy?, etc." *(Act out.)*

"Let's now be Abigail and Mark's hands and fingers taking objects out of a box."

(In advance of the lesson, prepare index cards with the names of objects written on them, such as marbles, a yo-yo, a basketball, nail polish, typewriter, a balloon, etc. Put the cards in a box. Decorate the outside of the box with pictures of mimes, if you'd like.

One at a time, a student selects a card, pantomimes taking the object out of the box, uses the object, and puts it back into the box.

When the child has finished pantomiming, ask the class to guess what the object was. What details showed what the object was? If it is not clear, challenge the actor to add a detail.)

"Let's act out now all the other things Mark and Abigail's hands and fingers can do." *(Elicit ideas from class, and pantomime.)*

Follow-up activities

1. Write poems about different people's hands. *(Pantomime)*

2. What can you do with your feet, your nose. *(Pantomime)*

3. Teach American Sign Language.

4. Make fingerprint pictures.

5. Use the Lawrence Hall of Science GEMS (Great Explorations in Math and Science) Fingerprint Unit to study fingerprints.

6. Refer to the Bibliography for resources for additional pantomime activities.

Abigail's Fingers

(In *Fingers are Always Bringing Me News* by Mary O'Neill)

One day Abigail said
In surprise:
"My fingers are almost
The same as my eyes.
Fingers are always
Bringing me news
Toes never know
Because of shoes.
They tell me what
Is hot and cold,
And what is too heavy
For me to hold.
They lift my crayons,
Smooth my hair,
And tuck me into
My underwear.
They hang my clothes
On proper hooks,
Put things into and
Out of pocketbooks.
They tell me what
Is soft and hard
And help me write
A postal card.
They know the rough
Of brick and log
And that softest thing
Is fog."

Mark's Fingers

(In *Fingers are Always Bringing Me News* by Mary O'Neill)

I like my fingers
They grip a ball,
Turn a page,
Break a fall,
Help whistle
A call.
Shake hands
and shoot
Rubber bands.
When candy is offered
They take enough.
They fill my pockets
With wonderful stuff,
And they always tell me
Smooth from rough.
They follow rivers
On a map,
They double over
When I rap,
They smack together
When I clap.
The button buttons,
Tie shoelaces,
Open doors to
Brand new places.
They shape and float
My paper ships,
Fasten papers to
Paper clips,
And carry ice cream
To my lips...

Casey at the Bat

HAVE YOU EVER
hoped so much for something and then been disappointed?

(Read the poem, "Casey at the Bat.")

"Let's start with a conflict where you want to go to a baseball game on a school night."

"It is *the* game of the season, a championship game, and your friend's parent has an extra ticket. It's the week before final exams, and your parent will not let you go."

"Who wants to play the child? The parent?" *(Role play.)*

(Side coaching: really persuade, convince, give reasons, work out deals, solutions, etc.)

"Now, let's change the conflict. This time you are a family with two brothers or sisters. One wants to go the football game, and one wants to go to the baseball game, and your parents have said you have to go together. Who wants to be the two siblings?"

(Role play.)

"Now, one of you is an older sister or brother who is totally uninterested in baseball and you have already made plans to meet your friends at the mall (or bowling, etc.). Your parents, who were supposed to take your younger brother or sister to the Casey championship baseball game for her/his birthday, are sick, and can't go. Your parents want you to take her/him so s/he won't be disappointed. (You are the only two children in the family.)"

(Role play.)

"Now, you're on line at the box office for the championship game. You're with two other friends, and you get to the box office window and there's only one ticket left."

(Role play.)

"Now, you get to the reserved seat section, and someone else was sold the same seat that you were sold, and there's not one empty seat anywhere."

(Role play.)

"Now, you're watching the game and your brother or sister spills soda all over your new sweater."

(Role play.)

"Now, they're selling "Mighty Casey" (the star player) sweatshirts. They cost $20 and you really want one. All your friends have one. Try to convince your parent to buy one for you. (Parent, your child has several sweatshirts already. You do not feel s/he needs any more.)"

(Role play.)

"Now, let's switch to the dug out. There's conflict in the dug out. One player wants to bat before one of the other players, or wants to play a position other than what the coach has him designated for."

(Role play.)

"Now, you are an injured player. The coach has instructions from the manager not to let you play. You're the best player and the team is losing. Convince the coach to let you play."

(Role play.)

"Now, there is conflict in the stands. Two employees both want to sell their refreshments to the same section. (It's the most profitable section.) Convince each other."

(Role play.)

"Can you think of any other conflicts that could occur either before, during, or after a great baseball game?"

(Discuss ideas, select, then role play.)

"Now, let's get to the game. All different kinds of characters come to a baseball game. Let's think about how these different characters might hand the ticket taker a ticket, go to their seats, and act at a baseball game." *(Have the children lined up and ready to go.)*

"Who wants to be a complainer? OK, let's see you enter and take your seat. Let's hear what you're thinking as you sit down and look around. Then, FREEZE, and the next person goes."

(Repeat this, each kind of character enters, takes a seat, lets us hear his/her thoughts, then freezes, so that the focus is on the next character.)

"Let's get some ideas for characters."

(Some suggested characters might be:)

> gossip
> mayor of the town, proud and pompous
> famous retired ball player
> President of the United States of America
> famous actor, very vain, very impressed with fame
> a pessimist
> an optimist
> a hassled parent
> a mischievous, bratty child
> an anxious 6 year old who's never been to a game before
> bored teen who had to take little brother or sister
> news reporter on the first day on the job, wants to get everything right
> an enthusiastic athlete
> cool kids
> very neat and efficient business man or woman who doesn't like baseball but had to take child for birthday—child is dropping ice cream, etc.
> enthusiastic parent with bored child who'd rather be watching TV
> the proud, bragging mother of Casey, the star player
> wealthy and refined man or woman placed in wrong seat next to some rowdies
> Casey's jealous sister or brother

(You may choose to interview each one to hear their thoughts as they come in and sit down.)

"Now, we're going to act out the poem in pantomime while I read it again."

"Who wants to be the players? The spectators? etc."

(Set the whole scene, and as you read it, they will mime it.)

"Well, the game's over. Let's now interview people to see how they feel. How will they deal with their disappointment? Fans, Casey, the coach, etc., may all express their disappointment differently. Do they make excuses? Do they get angry? Do they look ahead to a better game next time? Do they feel discouraged? Compare to some of your own situations where you've been disappointed."

Follow-up activities

1. Write an original mock epic heroic poem, individually or as a group.

2. Write the news article that tells how Casey won (instead of lost!).

3. Write a poem about a sports game of any kind.

4. Do the news broadcast for TV.

5. Design a Casey T shirt or hat.

6. Create a new product to sell at the next Casey game.

7. Divide the class into groups of 4 or 5. Each group is responsible for a different section of the poem, and prepares it in a different style that they choose, such as: rap, opera, rock, etc.

8. Write a poem entitled "Disappointment."

Where the Wild Things Are

(by Maurice Sendak)

HAVE YOU EVER
woken up in the morning on the wrong side of the bed, and no matter what you do, everything goes wrong, and you just seem to get into trouble for whatever you do?

"I have a story here where a boy named Max gets into trouble, and here's what happens..." *(Read story.)*

"Now let's think. What are some of the things Max could get into trouble for in the morning getting ready for school?"

(Elicit responses, such as doesn't like clothes put out for him, drops cereal on the floor, fights with sister or brother, etc.)

"Let's improvise some of these ideas." *(Role play.)*

"Now, let's see what trouble Max could get into on the school bus. What ideas do you have?"

(Elicit responses, such as opens the windows, takes someone's lunch, stands up, someone tells on him, etc.)

(Role play. Set scene with bus driver and two or three students. Combine all ideas, or have class select one they want to role play.)

"Now, Max is at school. What could Max get in trouble for in the classroom?"

(Elicit ideas, such as forgot his homework, pencil flies across the room by mistake, etc.)

(Role play.)

(Hint for role playing: If the scene needs focus, you can step in as the adult figure, or any other character, with a question or statement, etc.)

"Now it's dinner time. What trouble can Max get into at the dinner table?"

(Elicit ideas, such as feeds the dog food, kicks sister under the table, etc.)

(Role play.)

"Finally, Max is sent from the dinner table." *(Improvise the scene.)* "He goes to his room. He overwinds his alarm clock, throws his teddy bear on the floor, etc. This is not the first time he's done this to his poor belongings, but tonight the objects have decided to get even with Max. They have made a plan. When Max goes to sleep, they are, one at a time, going to come to life and scare him."

"Let's have different objects—what will you be? (lamp, clock, coat rack, teddy bear, bedpost, etc.) Think about how each object would scare him. What could the lamp do?" *(Turn on and off. The teddy bear could growl, etc.)*

"Think about how you, the object will become 'larger than life.' What sounds could you make? What words might you speak? And, as soon as Max's mother comes into the room, you will freeze back into your spot. That gets Max into even more trouble."

(Establish the order in which the children will come alive, and what they will do.)

(Choose a Max.)

(Teacher or student plays role of mother or father, and speaks:)

"OK, Max, now up to sleep. You've gotten into enough trouble today. I don't want to hear from you again. Understand?"

Max: "OK" *(He goes to sleep.)*

"First the _____ comes alive."

Max: "Mommy, help" etc.

(Parent enters the room. Sample responses:)

"Max, stop playing games. You've been in enough trouble today. Go to sleep."
"Maybe it's a bad dream."
"I'll leave the light on."
"Max, are you playing with the lights again?"
"Maybe it's the wind blowing in the trees?," etc.

(Repeat until each child has a turn being an object and coming to life to scare Max, if interest permits. After each of the children have finished, go back to the story, to the part where a forest grows in Max's room.

Have all the children in a special space being objects in the room. They become the trees— turn into the boats—turn into the Wild Things as you read the story description and the students act it out. The students may want to act out a scene before Max arrives, where the Wild Things are playing their favorite game, eating their favorite food, etc. Students decide what these foods and games would be, and how the Wild Things would eat, play, etc. Suddenly, the Wild Things see Max's boat approach. What would their reaction be? Continue reading the story from the part where Max sends the Wild Things to bed.)

"How would Wild Things sleep? Show me."

"In the story, Max becomes lonely. Have you ever felt lonely? Everyone in your special space, and show me how you sit when you're lonely. One at a time, tell me what you miss most back home." *(I wish I...)*

"Well, Max has decided he's going back home. Have Max wake up all the wild things, and announce his decision. One at a time, each wild thing must try to convince Max to stay. Focus students on how we persuade. Challenge them to come up with reasons that have not been used."

"What else could you say to convince Max?" *(Sample responses: we love you, we'll build you a palace, we'll be sick without you, who would take care of us, we'll be your slave.)*

(As tempting as each one is, have Max say "no," so that the students have to continue to persuade and think. You may choose to act out what would have happened if Max had said yes, either here, or after the story sequence is completed.)

(Narrate or read the rest of the story as children go from being Wild Things to boats, to trees, back to objects in the room.)

"Max wakes up as if from a terrible nightmare."

(Teacher comes in as parent, and pantomimes carrying a bowl of hot soup.)

"Oh, Max, I'm sorry you had such a terrible nightmare. Here's some hot soup I saved for you. I'm sorry you had such a rough day," etc.

(Have all the children pantomime drinking the nice hot bowl of soup and show how much better they feel now.)

(Alternate endings: Elicit from the class other endings for the story, and act them out. (Max decides to stay. What happens next? etc.)

Follow-up activities

1. What things make you feel better? Pantomime or discuss responses.

2. Read other "nightmare" stories such as *Alexander's Terrible, No Good Horrible Day.*

3. If you could escape to a place in dreams, as Max did, where would it be, what would it be like. Discuss or act out.

4. Make masks of wild things.

5. Use plastic from six packs of soda to make "Magic Glasses" that take you wherever you want to go. Tell or dramatize where you go and what happens there.

6. Make an entry into Max's diary telling about his day. Combine entries into a booklet. Are there any good days?

7. Write a Wild Thing's diary. Include entries about Max's arrival and departure.

8. Write a story to explain who the Wild Things are, and where they come from.

9. Make up a Wild Thing book of manners. Write and illustrate rules for proper game playing, eating, dancing, etc.

10. Make up a Wild Thing town newspaper. Write the news articles, ads, comics, horoscopes, etc.

11. Write and/or act out a description of a bad day *you* once had, and how you solved your dilemmas, or how your day ended.

12. You are a wild thing. It's been one month since Max left, and you miss him. Write him a letter. You may want to persuade him to return for a visit.

The Grasshopper and the Ant

(by Aesop)

HAVE YOU EVER wanted or needed something really badly, but you were not able to convince anyone to give you what you wanted?

"Well, here's a story in which the ability to convince someone meant life or death. It's called 'The Grasshopper and the Ant,' by Aesop."

"It's a special kind of story, called a fable. A fable is a story that has a moral, or a lesson, at the end. Animals take the parts humans usually would play."

(Read or tell the story. We have a favorite version, by Roberta Sewal, illustrated by M. Boutet de Monvel. After reading the story discuss what the moral is.)

"In our story, there are characters with different personalities.

>There is a grasshopper, who is a happy-go-lucky dreamer.
>And there is an ant who is an industrious, hard-working 'doer.'
>The grasshopper likes to stroll around and sing, smell the flowers, admire the scenery.
>The ant is always thinking of how much s/he has to do before s/he can relax.'

"Now, before we act out the story, let's try different pantomimes of how opposite types of characters would go about performing tasks. How would the industrious ant rake leaves, compared to the grasshopper? Gather seeds, etc."

(Children make suggestions and one at a time pantomime.)

"Now, let's try different ways of walking."

"The grasshopper likes to stroll around and sing. Think of the grasshopper's mood as s/he strolls around. What modern day song might s/he be singing as she strolls." *(Children frequently suggest "In Your Easter Bonnet," or "Memories" from Cats.)*

"Who would like to be the grasshopper and stroll around?"

(The grasshopper strolls as class hums or sings music decided on.)

"Let us hear what the grasshopper might be thinking or saying as s/he strolls around."

"Now let's see the difference between strolling and scurrying. Who would like to be the ant? What modern day song might we sing for the ant as she scurries around?" *(Children frequently suggest "I'm Late, I'm Late" from Alice in Wonderland.)*

"Let's sing (or hum) the music we decided on as the ant scurries around doing her chores. What words might the ant be saying to him/herself as s/he scurries around?"

"Now, let's act out the story. Who would like to be a grasshopper? An ant?" *(Choose different children to be the characters.)*

"I'll be the narrator. You do your parts as I tell the story."

"All summer, the grasshopper strolled around and sang. She did nothing to prepare for the cold winter ahead."

"Let's see the grasshopper doing some strolling around in a leisurely way. Let's sing for her."

"Now let's see the contrast of the ant busily working. She's getting ready for winter. Let's sing for the ant as she pantomimes different chores."

"Ant, freeze in your little house."

"Grasshopper, you suddenly realize that winter is coming. Let's hear out loud what the grasshopper is thinking."

"As winter draws near, she visits the ant to beg for help."

"Grasshopper goes to the ant's house and asks for food and shelter. Let's hear what the grasshopper says."

"The ant refuses. Let's hear what the ant says."

(You may choose to have all the children get into groups of three: grasshopper, ant and narrator, rehearse the scene, and play it for the others. Or you may choose to have the class as a whole brainstorm for other ideas to convince the ant, and act them out. Have the children consider why it was so important for the grasshopper to succeed.)

"Now it is spring. The grasshopper, hungry and cold, has died on the doorstep of the ant's house. Ant doesn't know this until she notices it's spring, and comes out of her house after the long winter is over."

"Ant, show us how you react. What are your thoughts now that you see the consequences of failing to help the grasshopper?"

"Here's a reporter from the local paper." *(Teacher plays role.)*

"Ant, I understand that you have just called the police because you discovered the body of the grasshopper on your front steps. Could you please tell us how you feel about the discovery and about what happened? If you had it to do over again, knowing that if you didn't help, the grasshopper would die, what would you do?" *(Many of the ants in the crowd can also react to the reporter.)*

"Let's have a dream sequence here, where the ant and the grasshopper reenact the persuading scene, and the ant allows herself to be persuaded. What will she accept as a good enough reason or bargain?"

(Students may want to stop here to discuss if living things in need have an obligation toward each other. Included in the discussion could be: What part did the grasshopper play in his own death? Are there people like the grasshopper? What does society do to help them? Was the grasshopper really doing nothing? Suppose the ant agreed to help, and next fall the same thing happened?)

"Now, we're going to have a trial. The ant is charged with contributory negligence in the death of the grasshopper. *(Negligence because she didn't kill grasshopper with a weapon, but should've known that turning the grasshopper away without food or shelter in the winter would cause his death.)*

"The ant is called to court to testify on her behalf."

"Ant, you are accused of contributory negligence in the death of the grasshopper. What do you have to say for yourself? Is there anyone who could testify on your behalf?" *(Students suggest witnesses who might support what the ant did, and play the characters.)*

"Here are some of the grasshopper's witnesses. Would you please share your feelings about the incident with us." *(Students suggest witnesses, and play the characters. The question may come up as to why they didn't help the grasshopper.)*

(The entire group becomes the jury.)

"Now jurors, how do you feel about what happened? Is the ant guilty or innocent of contributory negligence? What part did the grasshopper play in her own death?"

Follow-up activities

1. Students brainstorm for other situations in which someone needs to be convinced (i.e., children convincing parents, students convincing teachers, children convincing each other, etc.). They form groups of two or three and rehearse the situations, then perform them for each other.

2. Students become reporters and cover the trial. Using a newspaper format, perhaps a computer program like "Children's Writing and Publishing Center," They can create a newspaper covering the incident, and the trial. They can include interviews with the witnesses.

3. Students write their own modern fable using this or other morals. These can be collected into a class book, and form the basis of future dramatic experiences.

4. Teacher may choose to dramatize "The Little Red Hen," a story with a similar moral.

5. What would be some ways of describing the different ways the animals work? (i.e., neat and precise vs. sloppy and slapdash; happily and willingly vs. begrudgingly.) This activity can be used to teach adverbs.

The Emperor's New Clothes

HAVE YOU EVER
been afraid to admit the truth because of the consequences?

"I have a story about an emperor who loved clothes. In fact, he loved clothes so much that people were able to come from far and wide to sell them to him." *(Read the story.)*

"First, let's all get into our special spaces and pretend that we are very conceited and vain. Picture an imaginary mirror in front of you, full length, of course. Admire yourself in the mirror as a really vain person might. Try on different types of clothes."

(As the children are doing so, side coach as follows:)

> "Try capes, crowns, jewelry, etc. Focus on detailed and believable pantomimes. Feel the fabrics. Does something button, tie or zip? Think about the details and show them."

"Now let's get into pairs, and one of you be the mirror, the other the emperor. As the emperor tries on clothes, you, the mirror, let the emperor know how he looks." *(i.e. red is really not your color, that style is not you, wonderful material, etc.)* "We can switch parts after a bit."

"Now, let's take turns being this vain emperor and let's think of all the different characters who might come to sell him things. Where would they come from?" *(i.e. an alien, a Texan, a Paris designer, a punk, etc.)* "What would they sell? You might want to invent an original item of clothing that would tickle the emperor's fancy. Take turns with one child as the Emperor, and one as a vendor. Focus on really convincing the emperor to buy your item."

"Let's get back to the real story. One day, two swindlers come along, and convince the Emperor that they can make clothes that only people worthy of working for the Emperor can see. Who would like to be the swindlers: The Emperor? Let's act out the scene, and think of how the swindlers could flatter the Emperor and convince him."

"The swindlers begin creating their imaginary clothing. Let's hear what they're saying and thinking as they pretend to sew."

"All this while, the tricksters who are really making nothing for the emperor have been "sewing" most industriously. The emperor, very excited about the new outfit, sends in a variety of courtiers to see and report on the progress of his new garments."

"Let's come up with whom he might send." *(i.e. the court jester, a wise man or woman, the cook, etc.)* "Let's act out the scene with each of the characters meeting with the tailors. Let's see how each character debates aloud with him or herself about what to tell the emperor. Let's see how each one could convince the swindler to describe what they don't see. Let's see what (and how) the messenger chooses to report back."

"Continue to act out the story, but this time the *Emperor* goes to see the tailors. He realizes that he's been deceived. Let's hear the conversation he holds with two parts of himself—the liar and the truth teller—about how he should deal with the situation. One student can be the Emperor, and the rest of the class can try, one at a time, to convince him to either tell the truth or lie, and how to deal with his dilemma."

(End with the parade scene. Let each student decide on the character s/he will be at the parade. Let's hear what each character is thinking as the Emperor progresses down the parade route without any clothing! (You can use the conscience voices here if you wish— "tell" and "don't tell.") Focus on the moral dilemma each spectator is facing, and the response each finally gives to the truth the little child speaks. Perhaps the child's parents or friend try to dissuade him as they see that he realizes the truth and intends to shout it out.)

Follow-up activities

1. Have you ever known of a situation in which someone was afraid to admit the truth because of the consequences? Let's make a list of the situations, then we'll act them out. (i.e. a friend asks you how you like his or her haircut, and you don't, etc.) This can be done before the story as part of the introductory "*Have You Ever...*"

2. Have you ever had to write a thank you note for a gift you hated? Let's see what you say.

3. Read *The Principal's New Clothes*.

The Theft of Thor's Hammer

(Our favorite version is in *Norse Myths* by the D'Aulaires)

HAVE YOU EVER imagined what it would be like if your most valuable possession were missing?

"Let's all sit in our special spaces."

"I'd like each of you to think of what you consider to be your most valuable possession. Think of something that you value so much, that if you came home from school and found it missing, you'd do anything to get back. You don't even have to tell what it is. Just think of it."

"Now, imagine you've just come home from school, and discovered that what you value most is missing. Try to feel that emotion going up your legs causing you to rise to your feet. Feel it going up through your body, into your shoulder, your face. Show with your whole body how you feel. Show it with your hands, your fingers, your elbows," etc.

"Inhale an angry breath, exhale it like fire through your nose. Inhale, exhale through your mouth," etc. "Now magnify the feeling you just had by a million, and you've got the kind of powerful anger that mighty Thor felt when he woke up one morning and discovered that his magic hammer was missing."

"Everyone sit down while I read the story of "Thor and His Hammer" to you." *(If you read it in its entirety first, stop before the solution to the conflict. Or, you can read or tell it scene by scene and act each scene as you go. If you prefer, you can fill in the background without reading the story, and discuss who Thor is, that he lives in Asgard, his relationship with Loki, the special character of his hammer. You may wish to discuss what a myth is, and how they differ from country to country, culture to culture.)*

"Now let's start with the first scene when Thor wakes up and finds that his hammer is gone. Who would like to be Thor? His servants?"

"OK, Thor, react to your loss. Now command everyone to search under clouds, etc., for your hammer. Everyone look for it, and let's see how you react as you realize that you can't find the hammer. Think about how you will break the news to Thor. If you've ever had to break bad news to someone, think of how you did it. How did you act? Now in turn each of you will break the news to Thor, and let's see how he reacts." *(Act the scene.)*

"There is someone whom Thor suspects—Loki. Loki is still angry for the last punishment Thor gave him. Remember that Loki is mischievous, sneaky, fun-loving, but *very* clever."

(Have Thor call in Loki. Act out the scene from the story in which Loki attempts to convince Thor he did not take the hammer. He tries to convince Thor that he should suspect Thrym, the Frost Giant, instead of himself. Then read the visit to Freya and Thrym, and act out.)

Some suggestions for further expansion of the story:

1. Upon his return from seeing Thrym, Loki calls a town meeting of all the gods, goddesses and people who live in Asgard. The whole class participates in the scene. Some class members agree that Freya should marry Thrym, and some disagree. Have the students try to generate many ideas for solving the problem. Act out all the possible scenarios before returning to the actual solution of Thor disguising himself as Freya.

2. When Thor is getting prepared to impersonate Freya, he is obviously feeling very embarrassed and angry. Interview different people about how he's behaving. Possible subjects are his seamstress, his servant, Loki, and even his mirror.

3. Before Thor (disguised as Freya) and Loki (disguised as a bridesmaid) come to Jotunheim (Land of the Frost Giants), have a scene where all the jealous Giantesses are gossiping about Freya and her impending arrival at the castle.

4. Focus on pantomime as Thrym's kingdom prepares for Freya's arrival.

5. Reenact the banquet scene which concludes the story.

Follow-up activities

1. How could you solve the mysterious disappearance of one of *your* valuable or favorite possessions? Write an ad for a "lost article" column, or a news bulletin, or create a mystery story about how you found the missing article.

2. If you could own a magic item, what would it be? What would it do? Write the story or act it out.

3. How do you think Thor's hammer became magic? Write and act out the story.

4. What would have happened if Thor never got his hammer back? Write and act out the story.

5. What would have happened if Freya had to spend a day with Thrym? Write an entry in her diary about it.

6. What might have happened if Loki didn't agree with Thrym on the trade of Freya for the hammer? What other solutions might there have been?

7. Read and dramatize other Norse legends.

8. Have students research different Norse gods and goddesses and create a Myth Museum. The children are statues (or in tableaux), and when the visitors push a button, the statues come alive and tell their stories.

The Sun and the Wind

(by Aesop)

HAVE YOU EVER wondered how you could resolve an argument without physical force?

"Let's warm up for today's story by pretending to be different kinds of trees. Just as we walk, talk and act differently, depending upon the kind of person we are, we'll do the same depending on the kind of tree, flower, etc., we are trying to be."

"For example (everyone in your special space) when I beat the drum, let me see how you would use your faces and bodies to be the biggest, strongest oldest oak tree on the block. FREEZE. How would my oak tree get angry? FREEZE," etc. *(other emotions)*

"Now, let's see the difference if instead of the oldest, biggest oak tree, you were a drooping, sad weeping willow tree. FREEZE. What if my weeping willow tried to laugh? FREEZE," etc.

"Now what would it be like if you were a pine tree? The kind that makes a good Christmas tree. FREEZE. What if someone were tickling my tree? FREEZE," etc.

"In today's story there are also birds. Let's work as different kinds of birds."

"Show me at the beat of the drum what you would look like if you were an owl perched high on a tree looking out over all the other birds in the forest. FREEZE."

"What if instead of an owl you were a woodpecker who has found a good tree to peck at? FREEZE."

"What if you were a proud peacock? Walk around, show off your feathers. FREEZE."

"Let's be a tiny bird hatching out of his shell. Explore. FREEZE," etc.

"There are all different kinds of rocks. Let's be a big boulder. FREEZE. Let's be a tiny pebble. FREEZE," etc.

"Now, we're almost ready for our story about the sun and the wind. Sun and wind can do some very special things, and each does things in ways that are different from the other. Even if both do the same thing, like help to dry clothes, they do it differently. What are some things sun and wind can do?" *(Elicit examples such as:)*

> *Sun:*
>
> *make light in a room to save electricity*
>
> *solar heat*
>
> *dry clothes*
>
> *dry up puddles*
>
> *shine on a rock to show its beauty*
>
> *have barbecues*
>
> *dry your sweat*
>
> *help flowers, trees, vegetables grow*
>
> *make water warm*
>
> *melt ice, marshmallows, ice cream, snowmen*
>
> *cause sunburn*
>
> *eggs to hatch*
>
> *fade things*
>
> *make rainbows*
>
> *coax animals to come out of hibernation with its warmth*

Wind:

help kites fly

roll trashcans

spread dandelion seeds

blow sand on faces

freeze snowmen

cool us off

help birds fly

make hurricanes and tornadoes

blow hats off

blow leaves off trees

blow down trees

blow down nests

make flags snap and flap on flagpoles

make sailboats go

shape land by moving sediment

cool construction workers

air germs out of house

"In this story, the sun and wind have two different personalities. The sun is a very gentle, nice person. If s/he were standing in the lunch line and wanted to get ahead of you, s/he would probably say 'Excuse me, could I please get in front of you. I'd like to get to the computer room early.'"

"The wind, however, is a very different person. S/he's a big bully. S/he believes in pushing and shoving, and s/he would just push you and say, 'Hey, get out of my way, I'm here!'"

"Sun and wind liked to argue with each other about who was more powerful."

"Now, one morning, the sun and wind had an argument. They argued about who was stronger. The wind kept saying s/he was stronger because_____; the sun kept saying s/he was stronger because_____. "

(Pair up students and have them practice arguing as the sun and the wind. They each need to give reasons why. Have pairs present their arguments.)

"Finally, Mother Nature couldn't sleep anymore. The arguing was so noisy that she decided to send them traveling around the world to find an answer."

(Select a sun and wind, and group the remaining children into trees, birds, flowers, rocks, etc. Sun and wind will travel to each group and ask "Who is stronger?" Encourage each group to answer as the character they are portraying would do. i.e., the trees have to answer in terms of what the sun and wind do to them to show their strength: Sun, you make us grow, make our leaves look beautiful; Wind, you can blow us down, scatter our leaves, etc.)

"Well, they've consulted the flowers, children at the beach, rocks, rainbows, etc. No one can make a decision. Finally, they go to the birds. The birds can't decide either, but one of the birds has an idea for a contest."

"There is a traveler coming down the road. 'Whoever can make the traveler take off his coat wins the contest,' says the bird."

"Before we begin the contest, let's see some different kinds of travelers."

(Elicit suggestions, i.e. a happy little child, a proud king or queen out for a walk, a poor lonely beggar, etc. Act out the different travelers.)

"And now the contest begins." *(For the contest, everyone will sit or stand in a circle to be the wind and then the sun.)* "Remember, give the traveler room to act." *(Select one traveler for the contest.)*

"Let's see our traveler walking."

(You step in.)

"Hi, how are you? Nice day. Where are you headed?" etc.

"Suddenly the wind starts blowing, 'Ah, this will be so easy' said the wind. 'I'll just blow strong gusts of wind and blow that jacket right off.' He blew gently at first. Then harder and harder. At last, he blew a hurricane of wind. But the more he blew, the colder it got, and the *tighter* the traveler buttoned up his jacket."

"Traveler, let's see and hear your reaction to what's going on."

"Then it was the sun's turn. The sun, very gently, shone forth wonderful, gentle rays of warmth, until the traveler was so warm, he took off his coat. Let's see and hear the traveler's reaction now."

"Who won the contest? Why? What is the moral to this story?"

(Gentle persuasion is better than physical force—the sun was able to do with warmth and gentleness what the wind could not accomplish with force and anger.)

(Read different versions of the story.)

Follow-up activities

1. What other objects in nature could argue? Write a new story.

2. Write a new story with different characters and situations that illustrates the same moral.

3. Add music (Orff instruments) and create a play with a narrator to share with another class.

4. Find poetry about the wind and sun (to explore either before or after the story).

5. Write a conversation about what happened between Mother Nature and one of her *new* creations.

6. Have the traveler write a postcard to his or her mother or father telling where s/he now is, and what happened along the way. Be sure to have the picture side accurately reflect the environment s/he's writing from.

7. Create a "Mother Nature Mail Order Catalog" of things her creatures could order as protection from sun and wind. (ex: tree sunglasses, flower sprinklers, etc.)

8. What other ways could the disagreement have been settled? Discuss and act out.

9. Could there have been a different kind of contest? Discuss and act out.

The Peddler and His Caps

HAVE YOU EVER
been told to stop daydreaming?

"Well, I have a story about a man who was *always* dreaming *and* daydreaming. No matter what he did, or where he went, he daydreamed. Sometimes he even got lost because he just didn't have his mind on what he was doing."

"Sometimes, he was trying to think of new hats to create to sell. Before we start our story, let's see everyone in his or her special space. First, I'd like you to close your eyes and think about a special hat you'd like the peddler to create just for you. Think of all the things you might like to have him put on the hat. Would you like baseball cards all over it? Lots of ribbons and lace?" (etc., etc.)

"Now, open your eyes and you pretend to be the peddler. Think of the materials you need to make your hat. In pantomime, let's see everyone making the hat."

(Focus the students on details as they mime—) "Where's your scissors to cut out material? Where do you get it from? Let's really see the needle being threaded. If you are making a flower, let's see it. Be sure to uncap the glue before you use it.," etc.

"Now, one more warm up before the story. Everyone find a partner, and face each other. One of you is going to be the person looking into a mirror, and the other will be the reflection. Before you put on your hats, let's rehearse how this will go. 'Person,' move your hand up to touch your face. Go really slowly, so that the hand of the 'Reflection' can move at nearly the exact time as your hand, to do the same thing you're doing. Reflection, it's your job to watch carefully so that you can follow the Person's movements at nearly the same time the Person does them. Person, you must go slowly enough to let the mirror follow you. Remember, in real life, the person who looks in the mirror sees the reflection doing the same thing at the same time. Imagine how funny it would be if the mirror reflected what you did five minutes ago!"

"Now let's try a variety of movements, Person and Reflection. *(Act.)* Now let's try some different emotions. Person, look happy, sad, very conceited, angry, curious," etc. *(Have students reverse roles, too.)*

"OK, now we're ready to try on our hats, and look at our reflections."

"Person, you go first, carefully put on your hat, think about how you will hold it, and adjust it. Be looking at yourself in the mirror so your reflection can mimic what you are doing. Be sure to let your face show how you feel your creation looks. Now, let's switch roles."

"Let's go back to our seats. We're ready for our story."

(Either tell or read the story of the "Peddler and His Caps.")

"Let's start at the beginning of the story. Who would like to be the wife? Who would like to be the peddler? Let's see them sitting on their front steps, busy sewing and making hats. Let's hear what each is saying."

"At the end of the scene, the peddler announces that he wants to leave to sell his hats, but his wife is concerned he'll get lost. Let's hear his wife's concerns. He leaves anyway."

"Now, audience, the hats he sells are special. They are made of dreams. When a person buys a hat, he or she also gets to have a wish come true. If you are weak, for example, you become strong. Each of you, seated just where you are, think of a way you'd like to change physically. Do you want to become very beautiful or handsome? Very tall? Really muscular? Have magic power? Become an ant? Now pretend to put on a hat. Focus on your body. Feel yourself change. Slowly transform." *(Or, an alternative approach is to have each student come to the peddler as a certain kind of character, purchase a hat, and when the hat goes on, s/he transforms into a new character.)*

"Sometimes the peddler has trouble selling hats. People are reluctant to buy from him. Have the students create 'selling chants' to help the peddler, i.e., 'Hats for sale, hats for sale! Blue and red, brown and cream! Here's a hat to match your dream!' or, 'Hats for sale, hats for sale! Pink and purple, red and blue! I have just the hat for you!' etc. Let's have the peddler try to convince a passerby to purchase a hat. Let's hear from the peddler all the reasons why this person should buy the hat. Let's hear from the customer all the reasons why not."

"After the peddler sells all his hats he is very tired. He packs his bag, and starts to go home. Because he was so busy daydreaming, he is lost. Each of you get into your special spaces. Show with your body and face how you feel about being lost at night. Now show how you try to walk down different paths. The first one is very muddy, and the mud sticks to your shoes. The next path is mosquito infested, the next has very dense growth," etc.

"Finally, he sits under a tree to rest. Show with your whole body how you feel. However, little does the peddler know that a whole family of monkeys lives up in the tree! Let's hear the monkeys (in groups of four or five) discuss the tricks they plan to play on the peddler while he is asleep."

(Read or tell that part of the story. Have the children act it out, recalling the mirror exercise. Before focusing on the original ending, ask the children:)

"How would you like to see this story end?"

If necessary, you could ask:

"What could happen after the monkeys give him back his hats?
How could the peddler convince them to give them back?
What would a family conference of monkeys be like?
What would they plan?"

"Now let's switch to the peddler's wife. Whom might she call as she worries about where her husband is? Let's listen in on those conversations."

(Divide the class into groups to devise the final scene of the book. Have each group act out its version of the ending, or end it the traditional way.)

Follow-up activities

1. Design posters to advertise your hats.

2. Think of situations where you were daydreaming, and got into trouble. Act out.

3. Might the peddler ever change his ways? Write or act out "the further adventures of how the peddlar sells his hats."

4. Create a hat shop with hats for monkeys or other animals.

King Midas and the Golden Touch

(Use any version)

HAVE YOU EVER wondered what it would be like if everything you touched turned to gold?

"Well, there was a king, named King Midas, who loved gold. Next to his daughter, Marigold, gold was the most important thing in the world to him. Let's all sit in our special spaces and imagine we have just gone to the secret place where we keep all our gold and jewels. Let's count our gold, examine each piece, run our hands through it, hold our jewels up to the light. See each item. Focus on the details. If you take some jewels out of boxes, let us see you doing so with your fingers and hands. Assume the posture and character of a greedy person who just loves gold."

"Let's create a scene where the King decides to go to town to shop for some things. Where might he go? What kinds of items might he wish to purchase?" *(i.e., to the shoemaker for golden buckles on his shoes; to the pet store for a golden cage for his canary, etc.)*

(Focus on the characters and pantomime the scenes. Add words if desired)

"Let's go back to your special spaces. King Midas has now returned from shopping, and has gone down to his cave-like secret chamber way down in a dark, dark cellar. No one knows this place is there. Only one little ray of sunshine comes in through a small, barred window."

"Who would like to be King Midas? Let's see the King counting his money, gold and jewels. Let's hear what he is thinking."

"Suddenly, a strange sprite-like creature appears in the sunbeam. *(Choose a sprite.)* Let's see the Kings reaction. It approaches the king and says he can grant him one wish, and one wish only. Let's hear you, sprite. Midas is thoughtful, and turns several ideas over in his head. He says them out loud, and then thinks of reasons why each would not really satisfy him. At last, he says, 'I know! I wish that everything I touch would turn to gold.' Let's see Midas' satisfaction with his choice, and hear him planning how he will use it. The sprite tells him the wish will be effective at sunrise tomorrow, and leaves."

"The next morning, King Midas can't wait to test his golden touch. Let's set everyone up as a character or object that Midas touches. What shall we have?" *(Elicit responses, i.e., the door, the bedpost, the flowers in the garden, etc.)* "Midas, show how you react to the effect your touch is having on everything. Let us hear your reactions."

"Finally, Midas goes to eat his breakfast, but everything turns to gold. Let's see how he reacts, now."

(Set the scene with the chef, the waiters, etc. and show what happens.)

"What scenes would you like to add?" *(Elicit responses and act out.)*

"Just then, his daughter Marigold, whom he loves even above gold, comes in crying because all her beautiful flowers (etc.) are destroyed by being turned into gold."

"Midas is upset, and hugs his daughter. She, too, is turned into gold. Let's hear and see his reaction."

"What do you think happens? Let's brainstorm for ideas of how things could work out." *(Act out the various endings, then complete the traditional story.)*

Note: *(If you prefer, you can read the story instead of telling it in your own words.)*

Follow-up activities

1. The sprite sees ahead to the consequences of a golden touch and tries to convince Midas to choose something else. Get into groups of two and act out.

2. Pretend that the objects, animals, plants and people Midas turned into gold could still write. What story could they tell about the circumstances of how they got turned into gold? How do they feel about what happened?

3. What would you do if you got a chance to have a golden touch? Write or act out.

4. Read and dramatize the rest of the Midas story, in which he judges the music contest between Pan and Apollo, and receives his "donkey's ears."

5. You can use the sprite idea or a more traditional rendition of the story where the "wish granter" is Dionysus who grants King Midas' wish in order to reward him for saving his old friend, Silenas. Who is the sprite? Where did s/he come from? How did it get its magic. Make up the story(ies)." Dramatize.

6. What if Midas had wished for something else? What would it have been? Create the new story.

7. You are someone in King Midas' kingdom who was turned to gold. He's decided he doesn't like you, and doesn't want to remove the 'golden touch' from you. Try to convince him."

8. Interview people who were turned into gold. How did it feel? Did you still have emotions? Could you cry? laugh? feel hot or cold? Could you hear or see anything? Smell or feel hungry? Did you try to communicate with anyone? What was the sensation as you were "zapped" by Midas? What are your feelings as you get near Midas now? etc. (The class can make up questions and decide on characters they'd like to interview.)

The Three Billy Goats Gruff

HAVE YOU EVER
wondered what it would feel like to be a bridge, and be traveled over, day after day?

(Read the story. Proceed to act out the story focusing on the different way each Billy Goat goes over the bridge and why each is doing so.)

"Now let's hear the story from the point of view of the bridge."

"Hi, I'm the bridge. Not just any bridge. I'm the bridge that has strange trolls living under me, and three billy goats who are always trying to go across me. Did you ever think of what it's like to be me? I mean, think of all the things and characters that go over me every day and night. Oh no, here comes a person with a wheelbarrow filled with bricks. I hope I don't get one dropped on me—oh no—ouch!"

(Elicit from the class ideas of different things and people that could travel over the bridge. Have the children take turns being the travelers and the bridge. (Note: Rather than have the children walking on each other, have the bridge lie down, or sit, and the travelers "go across" behind him or her.))

"What might the traveler be saying or thinking as s/he crosses the bridge? Let's hear how the bridge reacts to the burden."

"Now we're going to have a bridge convention, with bridges from all over the world. (You, children, will be the bridges.) Would you like to tell us about the funniest things that ever crossed you? The scariest? The most unusual?"

"Oh my, I hear some knocking. It seems like the trolls want to tell their side of the story—what it's like to live *under* the bridge. Let's interview them."

Divide the class into groups (4 or 5) and have the students create a scene that focuses on the lives of the trolls. Act out the different versions. Do the same for the Billy Goats.

Follow-up activities

1. What if the goats didn't kill the trolls? What would happen next? Write a scene and act it out.

2. What is the next chapter of the story after the goats cross the bridge? Why did they want to go over? Where were they going? Create the sequel: "The Further Adventures of the Billy Goats Gruff." If interest persists, work on a class novel. Do the goats split up, for example, get jobs, find new friends, join rock groups, get married, etc.

3. Many years pass. The trolls move away. The Billy Goats move, too. Who are the new tenants under and near the bridge? Write or act out the story from the point of view of the bridge.

4. Before acting out the traditional ending: How could the Troll and the Big Billy Goat Gruff have solved their problem without fighting? Act out the solutions. Perhaps the bridge could offer solutions, too.

Pierre

(by Maurice Sendak)

HAVE YOU EVER known someone who does not care about anyone else's feelings? How does that make you feel?

"I have a story about a boy named Pierre, and Pierre did not care, at least until he learned his lesson!"

(Read Pierre, by Maurice Sendak.)

"Now, before we act out the story, let's improvise some scenes where different characters ask Pierre for some kind of help, and he just responds with his 'I don't care' attitude and phrase:

> A frustrated little sister or brother who can't tie his or her shoelaces, who seeks help from Pierre.
> A good friend who just had something terrible happen, and wants some help or advice from Pierre.
> A grandma or grandpa who needs to find glasses to read, asks Pierre for help.
> Pierre's toy robot asks for oil in order to function.
> A poor, sad, lonely, homeless person asks Pierre for some money.
> A lost child meets Pierre in a store, and wants Pierre to help find his/her mommy.
> A very patient teacher tries to help Pierre with his homework.
> Elicit other ideas from the class, and improvise the situations.

(Act out the Pierre story improvisationally.)

"Who would like to be the mother? Try to convince Pierre to eat properly, to go to town, etc. Who would like to be the father? Try to convince him to sit properly, etc. The Lion? Try to convince him to care."

(Or use the actual story as a script, with students taking the parts of narrator, Pierre, etc. Either way, before you get to the scene of the lion being taken to the doctor, stop the action and say to the character playing the lion:)

"You are the lion. Pierre won't come out of you. You are getting indigestion from this nasty little kid inside of you. Try to figure out a way to convince him to come out. Let us see what you try to do." *(Several other children may wish to try, too.)*

"You arrive at the doctor's office. Imagine the reactions of people in the waiting room, as well as the nurse, as a sick lion comes in. Let's have different people sitting there."

(Establish characters, and then act out the scene.)

"How should we have everyone finally get home?"

(Elicit responses.)

"Now that everyone's home safely, let's pose for a family portrait. When I beat the drum, in turn (number the children 1, 2, 3, 4...) come alive and describe your reaction to the incident."

Follow-up activities

1. What would have happened if Pierre didn't come out? Write that ending, and act it out.

2. Pierre is in the Lion's stomach. Using a tape recorder, have him narrate what it's like in there. (Or write about it.)

3. You are a lion tamer the day when the lion swallows Pierre. While you are trying to tame the lion, Pierre is in him constantly crying out, "I don't care." Tell about it orally or in writing. Act out the scene. How did this go from the point of view of the lion? of Pierre?

4. You are news reporter writing the action story for the day. Cover the incident.

5. Interview each character. Pierre: What was it like? Lion: What was it like? Parents: How did you feel when you discovered Pierre in the lion? Doctor: What was your reaction to the situation?

6. What happens next? How long does the lion stay with the family?

7. The lion finally returns home. Let's hear the lion's version of his visit with Pierre and his family.

8. Write a letter to Pierre. Tell him how you felt when someone didn't care about one of your problems, or didn't help you when you needed help.

Hercules and the Twelve Labors

(Any version)

HAVE YOU EVER
imagined or wished you were strong enough to lift even the heaviest of boulders?

"The title character in our story is Hercules. He is so strong that when he was an infant he was able to kill snakes with his bare hands. Today we'll use pantomime to act out the 12 labors."

"Let's all get into our special spaces to warm up. Let's imagine that we are each the strongest person in the world and we are entering a contest of all-powerful gods and goddesses. We have to lift a heavy, heavy boulder. Normally, it's not hard for us to do, but someone has cast a magic spell over this boulder, and it's impossible to move. Ready? Remember, there's no sound in pantomime, so you have to show all your effort in your body and your face. Figure out all the different ways you could move the boulder."

(Share additional background information on the myth here, e.g., why Hercules has to perform the feats, who he is, etc. Read or tell the story.)

(Have a different student each perform a different feat. Or, you can have the students stay in their special spaces, and do the pantomimes simultaneously. To start each feat, have Hercules' mean cousin, King Eurystheus, tell him his task; to end, have Hercules confront him with his success.)

"Who would like to be Hercules and pantomime the first of the labors?"

"Here is how you might describe the first task:

> Hercules had to take the skin of a fierce lion which was terrifying the people of the valley of Nemea. The lion's skin was tough and hard to penetrate. First, Hercules used arrows, carefully fitting each into his bow, and aiming. But the arrows couldn't penetrate the thick skin. Then he uprooted a tree to use as a club. What else could he try? Finally he killed it with his bare hands, skinned it, carefully, so as not to damage the pelt, and used it to wear as he accomplished his other tasks."

(Continue to pantomime the rest of the labors. Summarize each labor in your own words, or read from your favorite version. You can use the above format: The King gives him his orders, he completes the task, and returns to the King. Focus on Eurystheus. Let us see his growing jealousy and anger each time Hercules returns, successful.)

Follow-up activities

1. Create contemporary feats for Hercules to accomplish. How will s/he do them?

2. Create a class mural depicting the old or new feats.

3. Create a myth about the weakest person and his or her labors.

4. What might have happened if Hercules hadn't been successful at a particular task? Have the class create scenarios for "The Failure of Task One," etc.

5. Think of a very difficult task that you don't think you could accomplish. Send your problem to a "Dear Hercules" column. Have someone write, as Hercules, to give you advice on how to overcome your problem.

The Milkmaid

HAVE YOU EVER
been so lost in your dreams that you didn't pay any attention to what was going on?

"Once there was a girl who always was dreaming, She lived with her grandparents on a farm."

(Read or tell the story, "The Milkmaid.")

"Let's all get into our special spaces and let's think of all the different chores she might have to do on a farm: build a scarecrow, rake hay," etc.

(Elicit responses and then have everyone pantomime the chores in their special spaces. Experiment with incorporating different feelings:)

"Let's see you feeding the chickens when you're in a great mood; when you're sad; when you're angry because you'd rather be with your friends; daydreaming," etc.

Try adding different weather conditions:

"Let's see you scattering the seed to the chickens when it's windy; when it's cold; when it's hot," etc.

"Now let's each find a partner. One of you be a child, the other a farm animal. The child is always dreaming of escaping from life on the farm. Talk to the animal who's your friend. Tell that animal your secret wishes and dreams. Animals, you respond with sympathy, or anger, or any other emotion you think is appropriate. Give advice, ask questions, etc. You may choose to switch roles, if you like."

(Ask for volunteers to show their duets to the others.)

"Now, you can suddenly hear grandma (or grandpa) calling:

___(Name)___! You must finish milking that cow, and go to town to sell that milk! But...since you've been working so hard, you can keep the money for a special treat."

"On the way to town, carrying your pail of milk, you meet lots of passersby. Who could they be?"

(Elicit responses. Students act out encounters with different people and animals the milkmaid meets along the way to town. She might even meet various nursery rhyme characters along the way! Have each student select a nursery rhyme character and think of what s/he would do and say when meeting the milkmaid.)

"What other adventures could the milkmaid have on the way to town?" *(Elicit responses and act out.)*

"Now as the milkmaid is walking along, she starts to dream about the coming sale. She dreams about the farmer, who will give her chickens for the milk. Let's hear what she is thinking as she spins her daydream." *(Milkmaid "dreams" out loud.)*

"Finally, she imagines herself at a dance."

(Everyone in the class can, in slow motion, be part of the dream dance.)

"Let's find a partner. One of you be a child, the other a farm animal. Let's see you dance around in her dream as the milkmaid watches. First they play a waltz. La, la-la, la, la, la-la, la, la, la, la-la, la-la. Then a fast song. Then another waltz. What a lovely dance!"

"Meanwhile, the milkmaid, still holding her pail and still daydreaming, starts to dance to the imaginary music, slowly at first, and then when the faster music starts, more quickly. All at once the milk spills! She quickly comes out of her daydream and realizes that all her dreams are gone! Let's hear what she is thinking."

"What lesson does this fable teach?"

"Can you think of some other ways the fable could have ended?"

(Elicit responses, and act out the alternatives.)

"What do you think happens when she gets home?"

(Elicit responses, and act out the scenes.)

Follow-up activities

1. Make a song, speech or poster to advertise your farm products.

2. Write a modern-day version that teaches the same lesson. Or write the story set in the city instead of on a farm.

3. Create puppets, and put on a puppet show of the traditional or updated versions.

4. What if the milk were magic? Create the story using that change.

Nursery Rhymes

Humpty Dumpty

HAVE YOU EVER
wondered how Humpty Dumpty fell from the wall? What was he doing up there to begin with?
 (Read the rhyme.)
 "The King's court has decided to reopen the case and investigate the supposed 'accident.' They feel that he didn't simply fall off that wall. All of you will be the detectives on the case. What should we try to find out? Do you have any theories about the case?"
 (Elicit responses. (Possible areas for exploration: What was he doing on the wall? Was he alone? Who found him? What medical attention did he get? What kind of egg was he?, etc.))
 "To whom could we speak who might give us some information about these matters?" *(the guards, friends, relatives, etc.)* "Is there anyone here who can help us?"
 (Students work to produce witnesses and question them to see who did it. Have a trial. Favorite responses have included:

> *One child admitted he had done it because there were 25 rules in the kingdom, and one rule was that no one was allowed to be hardboiled and Humpty Dumpty had become hardboiled.*

> *Another was a theory that Humpty Dumpty was on a diet and sneaked outside to eat a cherry pie on the wall and lost his balance when he leaned over to get his pie as it started to fall.)*

Follow-up activities

1. Students take turns reciting the rhyme as different characters:

    as if you had just heard the news.
    as the queen, who is angry because no one was able to save him.
    as someone who cannot believe the news.
    as the nervous servant who couldn't help him.
    as a child who loved Humpty Dumpty.
    as a jealous king, who is happy to be rid of Humpty Dumpty.
    as a detective, who is trying to figure out the case.
    as a teacher who is explaining to his or her class what happened in history.
    as a child who has a lot of questions about the incident.
    as a news reporter.
    as a harried guard trying to keep curiosity seekers away.
    as the queen, trying to break the news to Humpty Dumpty's mother.
    as Humpty Dumpty's mother.
    as the doctor who examined him after the accident.
    as someone who is anxiously fearful that s/he will be accused of the crime.
    as the court jester.
    as an observer who saw him fall.
    as an opera singer who is told she must announce it to the audience.

    Brainstorm for other ideas.

2. Humpty Dumpty is successfully put together. But he isn't quite right. Brainstorm for situations in which Humpty interacts with other characters—and shows his new flaws.

Little Miss Muffet

HAVE YOU EVER
wondered what really happened between Miss Muffet and the Spider?
(Read the rhyme.)
"Why do you think Miss Muffet is eating her breakfast outdoors instead of inside? Why is she alone?"
(Elicit responses then act out each scene. Some reasons could be:)

> she's happy, it's a nice day, and she thinks it would be fun to eat outdoors.
> she's sad because a group of friends didn't invite her to their party.
> she's angry because she had a fight with her sister.
> she's disappointed because she couldn't go to a carnival. etc.

"Why does the spider come over to Miss Muffet?"
"How does he feel? What does he want?"
(Elicit responses and act out each scene. Some reasons might be:)

> it's too hot, so s/he wants to sit in the shade with her to cool off.
> s/he's hungry and smells the cereal.
> s/he's lonely, and wants a friend.
> s/he's mean, and wants to scare her.
> s/he's curious and wants to be close to her.
> s/he's scared of a big frog that wants to eat him, and wants protection.

"After Miss Muffet runs away what does the spider do? eat? cry? laugh?"
(Elicit responses and act out.)
"What happens the next day when Miss Muffet meets the spider again? Where does the meeting take place. What do they do? Create the story. Act it out."

The Three Little Kittens

HAVE YOU EVER
lost something, and had to tell your mom or dad?
"I have a rhyme here about three little kittens who had to do that."
(Read the rhyme.)
"How do the kittens feel?"
"How do you think the three little kittens lost their mittens?"
(Elicit responses and act out:)
 "Let's see each of you walk in and try to explain to mom or dad how you lost your mittens."
Some examples might be:

> in a mud puddle
> falling off their bikes
> a bully taking them away
> they were too big, and as the kittens walked in a parade and waved, they flew off
> chasing a mouse

they left them somewhere as the day warmed up and they took them off
they caught on the branch of a tree they climbed

"Now mother won't let you have any pie. Try to convince her that she should give you some.
"Wait! The kittens find their mittens. How?" *(Elicit responses and act out.)*

"O.K. Now you can have some pie! Let's first all be the mother kitten making the pie. *(pantomime)*. Now let's all pantomime eating the pie."

"Oh, oh! You're dirty! Kitten, try to break the news, one at a time, to mother kitten. Mother kitten, respond."

"Pantomime the kittens washing their mittens. How would they wash them? Dry them? What other ways could they get their mittens clean?" *(Pantomime the different ways the children come up with.)*

"Proudly show mom how nice and clean your mittens now are."

"How would you like to end the story?" *(Elicit responses and act out.)*

Follow-up activities

1. Design loss-proof mittens for kittens. How would they work? What would you call them? Create an advertisement, jingle and slogan to sell them.

2. What kind of pie would mother give to her kittens? Create the recipes for a "Cat Pie Cookbook." Be sure to include the ingredients, the method of preparation, and with what you think it should be served.

Twinkle Twinkle Little Star

HAVE YOU EVER
wondered what it's like to look at the earth from a great distance?

(Read the rhyme.)

"Let's have different people looking up a the star."

"Let us hear their thoughts as they look:

    a sailor
    an artist or poet
    an angry person
    a lonely person
    a happy little child

    What other characters could we have?"

"How do you think the star feels? What is it looking at? How much can it see?"

"Everyone get into your special space, and you'll all be stars. I'll be the moon. Each of you can tell me what you see and how you feel about it."

"Have you ever wished upon a star? If you could wish for anything in the world, what would it be?"

(Each person has the chance to make a wish. Act out where possible.)

Follow-up activities

1. The child in the poem wonders what the star is. What is it really? What would you like to pretend it is?

2. Make up a story about how the star got into the sky.

Little Boy Blue

HAVE YOU EVER
wondered what Little Boy Blue's problem was?

(Read the rhyme.)

"Where is Little Boy Blue?"

"What is he supposed to be doing?"

"Let's hear from Little Boy Blue how he happened to be asleep."

"Let's hear some animals in distress calling out to him. Let's see what happens as he doesn't come to their aid."

"How is he discovered?"

"What will happen to him?"

(Divide the class into groups. Each group can be responsible for a different scene: Why he isn't where he should be; What happens now, etc.)

Old King Cole

HAVE YOU EVER
wondered why Old King Cole was so happy? What could have happened to him to make him that way?

(Read the rhyme.)

(Elicit responses, some might be:)

> His wife just made him a new crown.
> He was just voted the best king in the world.

"Let's act out those scenes. What characters do we need? Who would like to play them?"

OR

(Divide the class into groups, and have the members of each group plan and work out their scene and present it.)

"Let's try some changes to the rhyme."

"What if, when the King called for his fiddlers three, they couldn't be found? How would the King react? Would he be impatient, worried?"

"Where are they? What are they doing?"

(Elicit responses and create scenes to show what would happen. For example:)

> They are frantically working on a new song for him, and are so absorbed in their work they don't hear him.
> One of them lost a fiddle, and is looking for it. They only know music for a trio, and don't know what to do.

"What would make you happy?" *(Act out the situations.)*

Jack and Jill

HAVE YOU EVER
wondered how Jack and Jill fell?
(Read the rhyme.)
"How do Jack and Jill feel when they leave to go up the hill?"
"Why would their parent(s) have asked them to go?"
(Elicit responses, and act out. Some ideas are:)

    Happy: They are excited to be home from school doing such an enjoyable errand.

    Angry: They were in the middle of a good game and their mother or father made them stop playing to do that chore.

    Adventurous: They weren't allowed to go up the hill, but decided to sneak up anyway.

"How do you think they fell?" *(Elicit responses and act out. Some ideas are:)*

    Trying to balance the bucket on their heads.
    Playing a game.
    Tripping over a rock.

"Now they have to go home to tell their parents why they fell and how they hurt themselves. How do their parents feel?" *(Elicit responses and act out.)*
"Let's hear Jack and Jill explain to their mother and father what happened."
(Maybe Jack blames Jill, or vice versa.)
"Let's hear the grown-ups reactions."
"How would you like it to end?" *(Act out.)*

To Market, To Market

HAVE YOU EVER
wondered what it would be like to do your shopping at a giant open-air market rather than a store?
(Read the rhyme.)
"What kinds of things are sold at a market place?"
"What kinds of characters could be doing the selling? The buying?"
"What sorts of things might they be saying or doing to attract customers?"

(Create a marketplace with all sorts of vendors and customers. See if some vendors can convince reluctant buyers to make a purchase. This activity can be used as a warm-up for the Aladdin marketplace sequence.)

Nursery Rhymes

Additional Follow-up Activities

1. "To teach rhythm and rhyme, have the students modify nursery rhymes, starting with a changed first line, and complete them with their own ideas, e.g.,

    Jack and Jill went down the hill
    ....

    Old Kind Cole was a sad old soul
    ....

    Humpty Dumpty sat on a wall
    Humpty Dumpty heard his friend call
    ....

    Little Miss Muffet, had a cat named Fluffit
    ....

    etc.

2. Have children make up stories about what happened before and after the actions in the rhyme took place. Have children design book covers for their stories.

3. For creative movement, have the children act out the variety of ways the characters could have moved, e.g., Jack and Jill *skipped* up a hill, *leapt* up a hill, *crawled* up a hill, etc.

4. Have children do choral reading of the rhymes.

5. Make a museum of Nursery Rhyme characters.

6. Tell the nursery rhyme from the point of view of one of the other characters, e.g., the spider in Little Miss Muffet. "I'm the spider Miss Muffet was afraid of. Do I look scary? Do you know why I was there? What do you think? Was it because I was lonely? Was there a frog chasing me?..." Have the class turn their collection of stories into a class book.

7. Have students make up nursery rhymes based on their own names, e.g.,
    Little Miss Marilyn, went out carolin' ....
    Jason, Jason, son of a mason ...

Aladdin

HAVE YOU EVER wished that you could have all your wishes come true? In *Aladdin*, Aladdin simply rubs a ring or a lamp and presto! all his wishes are granted.

"Before we start our story, we have to travel to a different land and to a time long, long ago. *(Hold up a piece of fabric or a large scarf.)* Now, close your eyes, board my magic carpet, and get ready to go! We're ready to start our imaginary trip. Hold onto your imagination, we're going way back in time... before cars.... before television.... *(supply your own ideas)*. Now let's travel in our imaginations to lands mysterious... far away... through places like, Arabia, Persia, North Africa, India, Morocco, Baghdad. Are you holding onto your imagination? We're almost there. Now imagine a a place of palaces, jewels, silks, princesses, sashes, pantaloons, turbans *(add your own descriptions—if you like, you can use pictures as you mention each item).*"

"And now, picture a poor ragged boy, turban on his head, and slowly open your eyes, because we have arrived in the land of Aladdin.

(The piece of fabric you have used as the magic carpet can be used in each scene for something different—a cloth to clean the lamp, mother's apron, a shawl for the princess, etc.—the class can help decide in each scene how to use it.)

"When we first meet Aladdin, in the folk tale, he lives with his poor mother. His father, Mustapho the tailor, died and poor Aladdin's mother was left with no money and her *very* lazy boy. He would do whatever he could to avoid going to the marketplace or doing work."

"Let's meet our characters. Who would like to be Aladdin? His mother?"

(Every time they play a role, they could put on a sash. Have lots of scarves or material available.)

"Let's have the mother try to convince Aladdin to go to the marketplace to get a loaf of bread for supper. Aladdin, think of all the reasons you wouldn't want to go *(too hot, too far to walk, too noisy, your friends are playing marbles in the street, etc.)*."

(In this scene allow Aladdin's mom to convince him, and let's see him go to the market, perhaps stopping along the way for a quick game with his friends, to daydream, etc.)

(Discuss with the class what a marketplace is like: its purpose, the kind of things that might be sold there, the kinds of sellers and buyers, entertainers, etc. Create a marketplace with the class, each person having a role.)

"Think of what you each might be saying or doing to lure customers to your booth or tent. If you are an entertainer or beggar, let's see what you would be doing." *(Have the children demonstrate individually, and then in a group to create a market scene, with Aladdin wandering around from group to group.)*

(After this first scene, focus on the introduction of the conflict in the story. This story lends itself very well to discussion of plot, structure, conflict, etc.)

"We've met Aladdin and his mother, two of our main characters, and now the conflict in our story begins. *(Define conflict if necessary.)* It is here that we first meet the evil magician who tries to convince Aladdin that he is his long lost uncle."

(From here, you can either tell the story scene by scene in your own words, or read from your favorite version, scene by scene. We alternate telling it in our own words and using books, depending on the scene. We have listed our favorite versions at the end of the chapter.)

Scene suggestions

Add a townsperson into the story from whom the magician can find out all he can about Aladdin before approaching him.

As each character is introduced, show illustrations of that character from several books so the children can see the variation in interpretation and illustration from version to version—a good introduction to the idea of a folk tale.

In each scene, focus on how the characters are feeling, i.e., when Aladdin is walking down into the cave, how would he feel? How would that feeling be mirrored in his walk, in the whole way he moves?

When the evil magician is chanting his magic words and sprinkling the powder over the fire, have the class make up their own chants, and in special spaces have everyone be the evil magician.

Have everyone pantomime Aladdin trying to pull up the stone with the brass handle.

Have Aladdin be accompanied by a good conscience and a bad one walking through the jewel-filled halls in the cave. Let's hear the dialogue as Aladdin deals with his temptation to take some of the jewels; as he recalls his uncle's advice: "Do not take anything, or you will die."

When the uncle makes his power work, and causes the stone door to the cave to shut, have everyone sit in his special space and imagine they are Aladdin, after three days of being trapped in the cave. As you point to each student, s/he speaks his or her thoughts aloud.

When the genie appears children can take turns playing the part, or the whole group can play it at once in their special spaces.

Before Aladdin returns home, there can be a scene between the mother and one of her friends in which the mother shares her feelings about Aladdin's disappearance and her concern for his whereabouts. The friend shares ideas of how to find him.

When Aladdin returns home (through the power of the genie), he tells his mother, in detail, what happened to him. Students can tell the story in a "chain"—one can start, then the next student picks up and continues, and so on. (Good for sequencing.)

Aladdin's mother plans to go to the Sultan to ask permission for her son to marry the princess. Have the mother share her feelings about the impending audience.

Stage the procession to the Sultan as the "80 servants carrying chests of jewels," etc.

Brainstorm the tasks of preparing the palace for the royal wedding. Each child can be in his or her special space pantomiming the actions the servants would be doing.

Have the students add a scene where the evil magician discovers that Aladdin is alive, married, and has the lamp. Brainstorm the ways he could have found out—through a magic crystal, an evil assistant, etc. Act out the scenes.

Brainstorm ways the magician can regain the lamp, before he decides on the plot to disguise himself and trade new lamps for old. Act out the other plans.

Have fun when the genie is transporting the whole palace, including princess and servants, to the jungle in North Africa. Have several students doing different things in the palace talking about the feeling they have as they are flying through the air.

Have students take the parts of people Aladdin meets in his 40-day search for the princess. What kinds of characters would they be? What would Aladdin ask each one? Where would the meeting take place?

The genie is appearing for the last time. The students play him in their special spaces. Challenge them to create new dialogue and a new kind of genie.

(Before acting out the traditional ending of the story (the poisoning of the evil magician), have the students brainstorm plans Aladdin and the princess could make to get rid of the magician and get the lamp back so they can get home. Act out these alternatives. Act out the traditional ending.)

Follow-up activities

1. What would happen if the genie did not appear when Aladdin rubbed the lamp or ring? Write the story this new way.

2. Create a story in which the genie of the ring tries to convince the genie of the lamp to trade places. Write it or act it out.

3. Read and act out other stories in *Arabian Nights*.

4. Create a story or play which explains how the genie got his power.

    Include an explanation of how he got into the ring or the lamp. Write it or act it out.

5. Write or act out the next adventure of the genie.

6. Write or act out what happens to Aladdin after this story ends.

7. With the students, divide the story into scenes. Have each group of students select their favorite scene to act out. Let them plan how to dramatize it. Put the scenes together with narration for a play to share with other classes. (Use student actors or create puppets.)

8. Create illustrations of the characters and incidents of the story.

9. Create a sequence chart or jigsaw puzzle of the story.

10. Re-write the story in story-poem or song form.

11. Where else can we go on the magic carpet? Have students create travel brochures or posters for the places.

12. What would you wish for if the genie appeared to you? Write a story or poem, or illustrate your wish.

13. Create a mural which sequentially depicts the story.

Story versions

Carrick, Carol, *Aladdin and the Wonderful Lamp*, New York: Scholastic, Inc., 1989.

Daniels, Patricia, *Aladdin and the Magic Lamp,* New York: Raintree Childrens Books, 1980.

Lang, Andrew, *Aladdin and the Wonderful Lamp,* New York: Puffin, 1983.

Pandora's Box

HAVE YOU EVER been so curious that you'd risk anything to satisfy your curiosity?

"Well, I have a story here that has some serious consequences as the result of what a curious person did. Before we start our story, though, let's imagine a box has been delivered to your house. You did not see the messenger, but you heard his voice and his warning: 'Never, never open the box, or evil things will happen.' Now let's have one very curious person who wants to open the box, despite the warning. And let's have a more timid person, who does not want to open the box."

(Have the two focus on persuading and convincing, coming up with reasons for each other why they should or should not open the box. What might be in there? They are not to actually open the box at this time. That will come later. Work with several pairs. Challenge each to come up with different ideas than the others did. At some point during each pair's work, you might interject—in a distant voice—"Do not open the box—evil will happen." Or, using a very coaxing voice—"Why not open it?" Have the student actors react to the voices.)

"Now we are ready to open the box. Imagine that before this box was opened, the world was a wonderful place with only goodness and good qualities in people. When this box was opened, out came all the evils we know in the world—pain, disease, jealousy, destruction, war, pollution...." *(Students can add to the list.)*

"Now scene by scene we will act out the story of how the evils got into the box. This story is a Greek myth, called 'Pandora's Box.'"

(Define myth, list the names of the characters in the story.)

"In our first scene, powerful Zeus, ruler of the world, looks down on earth from Mt. Olympus, and decides that earth is boring the way it is. He calls upon Epimetheus to go down to earth and create animals, and give each one a special gift for protection."

"Let's list gifts of protection for each animal." *(i.e., turtle's shell, porcupine's quills, snake's venom, etc.)*

"Who would like to be an animal? Which one?" *(There can be as many as there are children; work in special spaces. Animal noses or masks are fun to use here.)*

(Act out the scene. Epimetheus can decide how s/he wishes to create the animals and give them their gift of protection. Focus on each animal slowly coming alive, as if a sculpture could move. The scene concludes with Zeus inspecting the animals, or however the class decides.)

"In our next scene, Zeus decides that there should be man on earth—but not woman yet! So he calls Prometheus, and orders him to go to earth to create man. Prometheus does so, but he has no gift left for man's protection. He finally decides that fire would be the best gift of all for man."

(Discuss reasons for fire's usefulness to man: warmth, protection, light, to cleanse wounds, etc.)

"Epimetheus and Prometheus have a problem with endowing this gift. The fire belongs to Zeus, and is kept next to Zeus' throne. Epimetheus convinces his brother, Prometheus, to get the fire to give to man."

"Let's act out the scene. Who would like to be Epimetheus? Prometheus? Man?" *(Have several children play man.)*

(As they act out the scene, focus them through side coaching.)

"Prometheus, take your time creating man. Man, let's see you come to life slowly. Explore the world you've never seen. Use your five senses. How many things can you do with your hands, your feet, etc. After a while, let's see you get tired, weak, cold, hungry and frightened," etc.

"Prometheus, let's hear your thoughts on your creation. Now how do you feel as 'your man' tires. Let us hear how you decide to give him fire."

"Let's see Prometheus steal the fire from Zeus, and give it to man. Let's see man pantomiming how he will use it."

"In our next scene, Zeus discovers someone has dared to take his fire. He is furious. How do you think he finds out it was Epimetheus and Prometheus? Who would like to be Zeus? Epimetheus? Prometheus? Let's focus on Zeus' anger. Focus on Epimetheus and Prometheus convincing and negotiating with Zeus, trying to get out of being punished. Let's act out that scene."

"In our next scene, Prometheus receives his punishment. Zeus calls in Hephaestus, the blacksmith, the artist of the gods, and tells him to make the heaviest chains possible. He then has Prometheus chained to a rock with a vulture guarding him. It is the vulture's job to attack Prometheus' liver—which miraculously grows back each time. Prometheus is chained in this way for years."

(In a different myth, Hercules finally saves Prometheus. You may wish to interject this chapter here. If so:)

"Let's have five people as Hercules and five as Prometheus. Prometheus, *(in special spaces)* pretend that you are chained to a rock. Use your senses. Feel the rough rock against your body. Feel the hot sun beating down on you. Feel the rain on a cold, cloudy day. Hear the waves beating against the rocks, the sounds of children playing on the shore. Smell the food man is cooking with the fire you gave to him. etc. Use your five senses."

"Finally, Hercules *(each Hercules can save a different Prometheus)* comes and pantomimes killing the vulture, and releases Prometheus from his chains. Could there have been other ways to save him?" *(Act out.)*

"Now let's get back to Epimetheus' punishment. First, Zeus calls in Epimetheus, and tells him he is banished from Mount Olympus, and must to go live on earth among men. Epimetheus tries as hard as he can to change Zeus' mind, but to no avail. Zeus is determined to carry out his punishment." *(Act out.)*

"Then, Zeus calls in Hephaestus, the artisan of the gods, and tells him to create a woman. *(Some stories say out of clay, others out of fire, others out of opposites in the world. Let the children decide on how to create woman, and act it out.)* "Zeus calls her Pandora and all the gods and goddesses come to bring her gifts before Zeus gives her life."

(Have the group stop here—unless they've already done research on other gods and goddesses. Assign each student a god or goddess. They need to do enough research so that they can come before Pandora and present a gift that would be suitable from each. What might the god of war give? The goddess of wisdom? etc.)

"Let's act out the scene where each of you, gods and goddesses, gives to Pandora a special gift. Tell us what your gift is, and what you hope it will do for her."

"Now, Zeus, let's see you give her life. And, now you also decide to give her curiosity. *(Focus class on the importance of this gift.)*

"Who would like to be Pandora? Let's see you come to life, and begin to explore the world around you as a very curious person."

"Zeus then calls Hermes, the messenger of the gods. Zeus tells Hermes to deliver Pandora to Epimetheus, now living on earth, along with a box. Tell Hermes to warn Pandora 'never to open the box, or evil things will happen.'"

(Select actors, and act out the scene.)

"Time goes by, and every day, we see Pandora more and more eager to open the box. Epimetheus is certain that his punishment from Zeus is in that box, so he is unwilling to open it."

(Have the class brainstorm ways Pandora can convince Epimetheus to open the box. Have several students be pairs of Pandora and Epimetheus. Have them act out the ideas.)

"Pandora is now alone with the box. She's confused. She promised Epimetheus she wouldn't open it, yet Zeus gave her curiosity, and her curiosity is killing her."

(Let someone be Pandora, and have her conscience talking to her.)

"But, Pandora's curiosity gets the best of her, and carefully she opens the box, and out come all the evils we have in the world."

(Let each child decide which evil s/he wishes to be—lengths of dark fabric work well here as informal costumes. The children will emerge from the box one at a time as you tap each on the shoulder. As the evil comes out, it must do three things:

1. Freeze like a picture or statue of that evil. How would a selfish person stand and look? Would war stand big or little?

2. State what evil s/he is.

3. State what evil it will cause to happen as it escapes out into the world.

(After all the evils are out of the box, focus on Pandora, and Epimetheus, who has returned.)

"Let's see the scene in which Pandora and Epimetheus realize what has happened. How do they feel?"

"Let's hear Pandora's thoughts about what she did."

"Let's hear what Epimetheus is thinking."

(Pairs of students act out the scene.)

"Finally, they hear a gentle voice in the box asking to be let out. This voice convinces them to open the box once again, to release the last thing in the box—Hope." *(Elicit significance of this from class.)* "Hope tells them that although there will always be evil in the world, she will be sure that humankind always has hope."

(End as you wish.)

Follow-up activities

1. What gift would you have given man? Why? Write that story.

2. If you were Epimetheus who had to create animals what would you create? Describe it in writing, and draw it. Tour the "new zoo" of creations.

3. Find different versions of the Pandora's Box myth, and compare them.

4. Use clay or other media to create an artistic version of the scenes of the story.

5. Be reporters for the "Mount Olympus Times." Report on each of the major news stories of the myth. Look for human interest stories, too.

6. What if Hephaestus "goofed" and created something different than Pandora. What would s/he (it?) be like? How would the story have been different?

7. What if Pandora had never opened the box. Would the evils have found a way to come out? If they hadn't, what would the world be like today?

8. What else could have come out of the box? How would that have changed the story and the world?

9. Create your own myth about how something in the world came to be.

10. What might have happened if Pandora and Epimetheus didn't let hope out of the box?

11. How might the story have been different if Epimetheus created woman first?

12. What else might Zeus have asked to be created instead of animals? How would that change the story?

Daedalus and Icarus/Theseus and the Minotaur

HAVE YOU EVER had a parent or teacher warn you not to do something, but you decided to do it anyway?

"Here is a story in which not listening led to an awful ending."

"Daedalus was an inventor, engineer, sculptor and architect who made beautiful buildings, carved life-like statues, invented tools and instruments." *(Describe the character including any other details you would like.)* "But, he was too proud!"

"Let's all get into our special spaces and imagine we are inventors and builders. In pantomime, let's draw our designs, sculpt, build our models, etc. Let's see how proud you are of your invention."

"Now, Daedalus made some sculptures that were so lifelike that people thought they were real. Let's become some of the sculptures. Let's be a sculpture entitled 'The Happy One,' 'The Sad One,' 'The Thinker,' 'The Powerful One,' etc. *(Elicit ideas from the class and use the ideas for the titles for all to pantomime.)* Now, since Daedalus' character flaw was his pride, let's become a sculpture entitled 'The Proud One.' Slowly, let's see you become so proud of yourself that you feel like you're going to burst. Freeze. Now let's admire this sculpture: 'The Proud One.'"

"One day, Daedalus became extremely jealous, because Talus (his nephew and apprentice), was being showered with compliments on his work. Let's set up a scene where Talus creates a great piece of art. Different people (who shall they be?) come along and tell him how great it is. Let's have someone be Daedalus, standing on the side, eavesdropping, and reacting with jealousy to the comments. Let's hear what's he's thinking, and how he'd like to get rid of him."

"In the story, Daedalus is accused of throwing Talus off the cliff. *(Read or tell this part of the story.)* Let's have a trial. Let's try to prove Daedalus guilty or innocent. If he is found guilty, let's decide on a just punishment. *(Brainstorm to determine which characters each side would produce. Have the students improvise what each witness says.)* Daedalus, what can you say in your own defense?"

"Let's return to our story. In the traditional version, Daedalus is banished from Athens and sent to Crete. Daedalus loves Athens, and doesn't want to leave. Let's take turns being Daedalus trying to convince the King to permit him to stay. Daedalus is unsuccessful. Let's see his departure. Let's hear to whom and how he says good-bye."

"Daedalus arrives in Crete, where he is to take up residence. After a while, he is asked by King Minos to build a labyrinth, or maze, to imprison a Minotaur, a creature who is half bull and half man." *(Show the class some different illustrations of the Minotaur from several versions of the story.)*

"The character of the Minotaur in the story is an interesting one. But there's a part to this myth that involves another character named Theseus." *(Read or tell the story of Theseus, his arrival and slaying of the Minotaur.)*

"Now the character of the Minotaur is a very unusual one. I know that if you could ask him some questions, you would have some interesting ones. What would some of these questions be?"

(Record them as the children come up with them. Some questions students have asked, have been: Why do you eat people? Do you only eat once a year? Do you eat all 14 humans at once, or do you save some? Do you get lonely? What do you do for fun? Would you rather be man or bull? How do you feel about your mother and father? Have you ever tried to escape? How did you get your name?)

(Stop at some point and then let the class decide on other characters who could help shed light on the Minotaur's situation.)

"Class, if we could invite some other characters who could get the answers to our questions *(not including the creator of the myth)*, whom could we ask?"

(Some of the characters the students have used have included: a fly on the wall of the maze; the keeper of the maze; Zeus; the Minotaur himself (leave him for last, if possible); an intended victim who survived, Ariadne, etc.)

"OK, Let's start interviewing some of these characters. I will become one of the characters on your list who will visit you, a group of Cretan citizens, to answer your questions about the Minotaur. I will pretend to be one of them, and start to talk to you about the situation. As soon as you have figured out who I am, you may begin to ask me questions to help us better understand the Minotaur and the situation."

"Ladies and gentlemen, I am very grateful to have the opportunity to speak to you today about the Minotaur. I was present at his birth. It was remarkable how dramatic the situation became when I presented the mother with that extraordinary baby, half boy child and half bull. At this time, I would be pleased to answer any questions you might have for me."

(Teacher turns to class, and asks, "Who am I?") "Yes, I am the obstetrician who delivered the Minotaur." *(Teacher answers questions. Teacher creates the appropriate answers, depending on the facts of the myth and what seems right. At some point, you may want to stop and have students be the other characters to interview.)*

(At the end of the interviews, read the different traditional explanations of how the Minotaur came to be (such as Poseiden's curse on the wife of King Minos).)

"Let's act out the portion of the story where Theseus arrives in Crete, falls in love with Ariadne, and seeks Daedalus' help."

"How does Theseus kill the Minotaur? Let's act out his search through the maze, the slaying of the beast, and the escape of the killer with Ariadne." *(You may choose to read this portion of the story while the students act it out in pantomime.)*

"Now let's return to Daedalus. When King Minos realizes the role he played in assisting Theseus to kill the Minotaur, he becomes furious, and imprisons Daedalus, along with his son Icarus."

"Daedalus, remember, is very creative. What are some of the ways he could come up with to escape? Act out these ideas."

"Finally, Daedalus sees the birds flying outside the window, and gets his idea to make wings and fly away." *(Tell or read that part of the story.)*

"Let's get into our special spaces in groups of two, and work as quickly and as stealthily as we can to create our wings. When you're done, tie the wings on your son, and give him your advice about not flying too close to the sun."

(Read and act out the ending where Daedalus advises Icarus not to fly too close to the sun or too close to the sea. Read how Icarus disobeys his father's advice.)

"Let's take turns being Icarus flying. Let's hear his thoughts, one by one, about how flying feels. Let's hear why he decides to ignore his father's warning." *(You can assemble the rest of the students as a Greek chorus, calling out warnings to him as a group; or have them work in pairs to be the two parts of his conscience talking to him, one giving him reasons to follow his father's advice, the other giving him reasons not to.)*

"Let's see Daedalus and how he is reacting as he watches Icarus. Does he try to save him? How? Let's see and hear what he thinks and does." *(Have each of the Daedalus characters act it out.)*

"There are different versions of what happened after that. What do you think happened to Icarus?" *(Write and act out the story.)* "Where do you think Daedalus went? What happened to him?" *(Write and act out your ideas.)*

(Share with the class some of the traditional endings such as the one where he ends up in Sicily and enters a contest devised by King Minos.)

"Let's return to Theseus. There's much more to his story after he escapes."

(Teacher, you can either proceed to read and act out the continuation of the story of Theseus, or assign different groups to cover different parts of the story. Each group can research and make a dramatic presentation to the rest of the class in a sequential series: his birth, his acquisition of the throne, his rule as king, his return to Athens, etc.)

Follow-up activities

1. Were you ever in a situation where you were warned not to do something, but you did it anyway? What were the consequences? What could have been an alternative behavior? Brainstorm the situations, and act out the improvisations.

2. Be an inventor. Try to convince someone to patent your invention, or buy it. Create ads for your invention.

3. Is Daedalus to blame for Icarus' death? Take him to trial.

4. Create a museum of inventions mythological characters would use.

5. Create the Athens or Crete newspaper, with news articles or interviews about the Theseus and the Minotaur story.

6. Use *Reader's Theatre from Greek Mythology I* by Joanne F. Karr (Contemporary Drama Service, Box 7710, Colorado Springs, CO 80933), to dramatize the Daedalus and Icarus story. It is fun to use the script to do a "Greek Chorus," dividing the class into 3 groups and having the members of each group speak their parts in chorus.

7. Have the students solve the maze of Theseus and the Minotaur in *Storybook Mazes -23 Mazes Based on Classic Children's Stories* by Dave Phillips (New York: Dover Publications, Inc., 1978).

8. The stories of Daedalus and Icarus and Theseus and the Minotaur, and the characters involved in them, lend themselves to lurid articles for publication in a supermarket tabloid. Write the articles (King's Son Kills Bull-Headed Monster, Princess Has Own Monstrous Brother Killed, then Betrays Slayer, etc.), and publish the results.

9. The plots of these myths lend themselves to soap opera format. Write and act out a soap opera using the characters.

10. Read *Wings* by Jane Yolen (New York: Harcourt Brace Jovanovich, 1991). Use it as the basis of a choral speaking piece.

11. It seems that we have found fragments of the diaries of such characters as Ariadne, Daedalus, Theseus, and Dionysus. The Diaries have entries that would help us on our quest for information about the Minotaur. Brainstorm for the characters whose diaries would be helpful. Choose one character. Pretend to be that character. Think of a situation that happened, and write one diary entry about it, either before or after it happened, that tells your feelings as that character, about what went on. Remember, the character may have stopped to think as s/he wrote, so there may be appropriate doodles in the margins.

Then have the children read their "entries" aloud, one by one, character by character, and discuss the possible chronology of the entries that combine to make a larger section of each character's diary.

12. Did Icarus really die? Maybe he disappeared and reappeared somewhere? Where do you think he went? What do you think happened? Re-write the ending of the myth. Perhaps Icarus is with Amelia Earhart in a place for former flyers. Write the conversation they might have.

13. Have a panel of psychologists discussing whether Daedalus is to blame in Icarus' death.

14. Create a modern day myth with a situation in which a child does not listen to its parent.

15. Should Icarus have listened to his father? Set up a debate.

16. Children can design two different kinds of mazes for the various characters in mythology. One, which would be used to imprison a character. Would a maze to imprison Hercules be different from a maze to house Pandora? The other kind of maze is when you have to go from a starting point to an ending point. For example, can you get Pandora through a maze to Hope; or get Hercules to the golden apples?

17. Have the students use *Algernon,* a computer program by Sunburst, in which they lead a mouse through a maze using an elementary computer language.

The Library Sequence

HAVE YOU EVER wondered what it would be like to have the stories and poems in the library come to life?

"I would like each of you to decide on your favorite character from a story or poem. You are going to imagine that you are that character, in the book on a shelf in the library. I'll be the librarian, and will lock up the library for the night. Every time you see me lock the library door, it will be the signal for each of you in turn to come to life, speak and act as the character. Then, as you hear me come back into the library, hurry back into your book on the shelf and freeze."

"Take a few minutes to think of the character you'd like to be, and what that character would say. For example, if you're Little Red Riding Hood, what might you say?" *(Give students time to plan their parts.)*

"Let's decide on the order in which you'll each come to life. Are we all ready? Let's start."
(Create your own dialogue, or use the following as a guide.)

"Oh my, it's way past time for me to lock up this library and go home. What a hard day I had—I helped so many people, and put all the books in order." *(Teacher locks the door.)*

First character comes to life. Teacher gives child time to act, before returning to the library.

"Hmm, I thought I heard something on the way out. Maybe I left a tape recorder on in here." *(Teacher goes in to check.)* "Everything's quiet. I must be imagining things. I guess I'll lock up again."

Second character comes to life. Repeat as above, and ad lib as teacher. At one point one of the students can take the part of custodian or security guard (or other character) who unlocks the door.

Variations:

Instead of one character per book, have children form groups in which they are several characters from the same book, with the entire group coming to life at the same time.

Two characters from different books can come alive and have a dialogue. Students may wish to decide in advance who might be well suited to work together, and even practice for a few moments before the improv starts.

As a follow-up to student unit on biographies, substitute a Hall of Fame for the library, and have the teacher be the curator.

In October, as a Halloween variation, have each child be a witch from a different story i.e., Frog Prince, Snow White, Hansel and Gretel, etc.

Follow-up activities

1. Several characters from different books are a family. They are eating a meal together. What would each say during the meal? How would each behave at the table? Act it out.

2. Characters from different stories give each other advice based on their experiences. Little Red Riding Hood can advise the Three Little Pigs about wolves, for example.

3. Have students create larger than life-sized book covers from which they can emerge. This could be developed into a play for National Library Week.

Bibliography for Drama

Allen, June. *The Other Side of the Elephant,* Buffalo, NY: DOK Publishers, 1977.

Cranston, Jerneral W. *Transformations Through Drama-A Teacher's Guide to Educational Drama K-8,* Lanhan MD: University Press of America, 1991.

Cresci, Maureen McCurry. *Creative Dramatics for Young Children,* Glenview, IL: Scott Foresman & Co., 1989.

Davies, Geoff. *Practical Primary Drama,* London: Heinemann Educational Books, 1983.

Fox, Mem. *Teaching Drama to Young Children,* Portsmouth, New Hampshire: Heinemann, 1987.

Hamblin, Kay. *Mime, A Playbook of Silent Fantasy,* Garden City, NY: Doubleday & Co., 1978.

Lipson, Greta Barclay. *Famous Fables for Little Troupers*, Carthage, IL: Good Apple Publications, 1984.

Nobleman, Roberta. *Mime and Masks*, Rowayton, CT: New Plays Books, 1979.

Novelly, Maria, C. *Theatre Games for Young Performers*, Colorado Springs, CO: Meriwether Publishing Ltd., 1985.

O'Neill, Cecily and Alan Lambert. *Drama Structures,* Century Hutchinson, Ltd., London, 1989.

Polsky, Milton. *Let's Improvise,* Englewood Cliffs, NJ: Prentice-Hall, Inc., 1980.

Spolin, Viola. *Improvisation for the Theatre,* Evanston, IL: Northwestern University Press, 1963.

Swartz, Larry. *Drama Themes*, Markham, Ontario: Pembroke Publishers, Ltd., 1988.

Ward, Winifred. *Playmaking with Children,* New York: Appleton Century Crofts, Inc., 1957.

Ward, Winifred. *Stories to Dramatize,* New Orleans, LA: Anchorage Press, 1969.

Way, Brian. *Development Through Drama,* Humanities Press, Inc., Atlantic Highlands, NJ, 1973.

Wayman, Joe and Lorraine Plum. *Secrets and Surprises*, Carthage, IL: Good Apple, Inc., 1977.